TWAYNE'S WORLD AUTHORS SERIES

A Survey of the World's Literature

FRANCE

Maxwell A. Smith, Guerry Professor of French, Emeritus
The University of Chattanooga
Visiting Professor in Modern Languages
The Florida State University

EDITOR

Edmond Rostand

TWAS 420

Edmond Rostand

EDMOND ROSTAND

By ALBA della FAZIA AMOIA

Hunter College of the
City University of New York

TWAYNE PUBLISHERS

A DIVISION OF G. K. HALL & CO., BOSTON

Library of Congress Cataloging in Publication Data

Amoia, Alba della Fazia.
  Edmond Rostand.

  (Twayne's world authors series ; TWAS 420   :   France)
  Bibliography: p.   133 - 35
  Includes index.
    1.   Rostand, Edmond, 1868-1918. 2. Authors, French—20th cen-
tury—Bibliography.
PQ2635.08A4   842'.8 [B]   77-27245
ISBN 0-8057-6260-4

To the Romantic Positivist

Contents

About the Author

Alba della Fazia Amoia is an Associate Professor of Romance Languages at Hunter College of the City University of New York. She received her B.A. degree from Barnard College, and then went on to Columbia University to earn her Master of Arts, Master of International Affairs, and Ph.D. degrees. Professor Amoia also studied at the Université d'Aix-Marseille in France as a Fulbright scholar, and has taught at Barnard, Columbia, and the United Nations.

A recipient of research grants from the City University of New York and the American Philosophical Society, she has had the opportunity to publish numerous articles, book reviews, interviews, etc. in the fields of French and Italian literature. Professor Amoia has also authored *Jean Anouilh* (Twayne's World Authors Series), *Critical Bibliography of Jean Anouilh*, *The Italian Theatre Today*, and *Sixteen Unpublished Letters of Baron Grimm*; edited or co-edited at least seven other books, and translated two others: *Legal Effects of United Nations Resolutions* and Armand Gatti's *The Imaginary Life of the Street Cleaner Auguste G . . .*

Preface

Known both for his memorable dramatic works and for his patriotic war poems, Edmond Rostand (1868 - 1918) is one of France's great literary figures. His plays include *La Princesse lointaine* (*The Princess Far Away*), *La Samaritaine* (*The Woman of Samaria*), *Les Romanesques* (*Romantics*), the very popular *Chantecler* (*Chanticleer*), *L'Aiglon* (*The Eaglet*), which became an immediate success as played in 1900 by Sarah Bernhardt, and the posthumous *La Dernière Nuit de Don Juan* (*The Last Night of Don Juan*). His best known and most widely appreciated play, however, is *Cyrano of Bergerac*, which appeared in 1897 and has since been translated into practically every language.

Because his poetic production (*Les Musardises, Le Cantique de l'aile*, and *Le Vol de la Marseillaise*) contributes very little to the study of the real Edmond Rostand, I have compressed an analysis of it into one chapter. The poems are, in fact, highly perfected stylistic exercises containing only a few verses worthy of note. *Les Musardises* (1890), a volume of light and graceful poems presented to his wife, the poet Rosemonde Gérard, as a wedding gift, are noticeably evocative and even imitative of Victor Hugo and Alfred de Musset, Rostand's principal poetic models. *Le Cantique de l'aile* (*The Canticle of the Wing*), published in 1910, contains Rostand's best poems, including "Un Soir à Hernani" ("An Evening at Hernani"), which had appeared earlier, in 1902, on the centenary of Victor Hugo's birth. Composed in 1914, during World War I, *Le Vol de la Marseillaise* (*The Flight of the Marseillaise*) reflects a particular mood: the poet's sorrow and pain due to his inability to serve his country and contribute personally to preventing its devastation. The lines Rostand wrote during those difficult times are not true poetry but rather the unburdening of a soul handicapped by external realities and physical limitations. Although its title implies soaring flight, the poems contained in *The Flight of the Marseillaise* are weighed down by dark and impure elements. Rostand's poetry has not, in fact, withstood the test of time except in his dramas.

On the other hand, Edmond Rostand's spiritual development can be traced through an analysis of his dramatic works, and this is the aim I have set for myself in the present volume. His plays are examined here in chronological order in the belief that such a presentation is best suited to a study of the playwright's spiritual evolution.

Technically speaking, Rostand's theater is unique in the second half of the nineteenth century, thanks to a mixture of Romantic preciosity and heroic epic style perfectly suited to the stage. His dramatic production may be seen as a form of ego cult, sometimes highly exaggerated, often affected and ironic, and always theatrical and histrionic. For this reason, Rostand's theater was evaluated in 1910 as a skillful "playing" technique (*le jeu*), and the dramatist was accused of shunning simple, serene Beauty. Although he was accorded honors as a *poet*, Rostand was denied the title of *writer*.[1] After his death, however, the public began to catch sight of something more profound, more human, and more eternal in his work. His ideas may be outdated today, but his soul is ever alive for those who are sensitive and sympathetic to his works and to the eternal sentiments expressed by his characters.

From *Romantics*, published in 1894 in Rostand's youth, through the masterpieces of his maturity (*Cyrano* in 1897 and *The Eaglet* in 1900), and on to his winter of despair (*Don Juan*, written in 1910 and published posthumously in 1921), the cycle of Rostand's life—his hopes, aspirations, and disillusionment—can be traced. Even though disillusioned, however, Rostand, like the rooster of his creation, Chanticleer, still strove in *Don Juan* toward an ideal—an ideal perhaps less Romantic, less affected than in his previous plays, but certainly just as noble and heroic: facing life courageously.

The sections of this volume are divided thus: a short chronology of the significant dates and facts of Rostand's biography and publications precedes a chapter sketching the life and times of the author solely as they relate to his work. The chapter dedicated to his poetry follows. The body of the book is devoted to analyses of the plays. The commentary on each dramatic work begins with a brief résumé of the plot, followed by a study of the most important characters and dominant themes. The concluding chapter of the book contains some brief stylistic considerations, as well as a discussion of Rostand's ideas, his art, and his influence. I have tried to demonstrate where his originality lies and to what extent and why Rostand still lives today. The simplest explanation is, perhaps, that the sentiments he expresses are eternal ones: love, love of country, the desire to *feel* useful and to *be* useful to others.

The English titles and quotations of Rostand's plays (with the exception of *The Last Night of Don Juan*, translated by T. Lawrason Riggs) are those of Henderson Daingerfield Norman. All other translations are my own unless otherwise noted. I stand fully ready to acknowledge Riggs' translation in *Poetic Drama*, edited by Alfred Kreymborg, New York: Modern Age Books, 1941, pp. 702 - 25, and Norman's two-volume translation of the *Plays of Edmond Rostand*, New York: Macmillan, 1921, since these titles have been acquired by persons who have left unanswered my requests for permission to quote. The titles of Rostand's plays and collections of poetry—except *Les Musardises* which cannot accurately and succinctly be translated into English—are given in both French and English in the Chronology, but in English only thereafter.

For having made the writing of this book possible, I wish to express my thanks to Professors Sylvia Bowman, Bettina L. Knapp, René Taupin, Sidonia Taupin, and Teresa Camporeale; to my editor, Professor Maxwell A. Smith; to Dr. Franco Amoia, and to Dr. and Mrs. Giuseppe Fiore.

ALBA DELLA FAZIA AMOIA

*Hunter College of the City
University of New York*

Chronology

the Théâtre Sarah-Bernhardt with Sarah Bernhardt in the role of the Duke of Reichstadt. Rostand retires to Cambo, in the Pyrenees, suffering from pulmonary congestion; the Legion of Honor bestowed on him, July 14.

1901   Elected to the French Academy, the youngest writer ever admitted, replacing Henri de Bornier; postponement of reception for reasons of health.

1902   Wrote "Un Soir à Hernani" ("An Evening at Hernani").

1903   Formal reception into the French Academy, June 4.

1907   Death of father. Undergoes surgery.

1910   Suffers a pulmonary embolism, January 24. *Chantecler (Chanticleer)* performed on February 7 with Lucien Guitry; meets with cold reception. Writes new version of *La Princesse lointaine (The Princess Far Away)*. Publishes *Le Cantique de l'aile (The Canticle of the Wing)*.

1911   Involved in an automobile accident. Revised edition of *Les Musardises* published.

1914   *Le Vol de la Marseillaise (The Flight of the Marseillaise)* published.

1915   Death of brother, January 20.

1916   Death of mother, September 12.

1918   Death of Edmond Rostand in Paris, December 22.

1921   *La Dernière Nuit de Don Juan (The Last Night of Don Juan)* published posthumously; produced in 1922; it proved to be a complete fiasco.

CHAPTER 1

Life and Times

EDMOND Rostand was born toward the end of France's Second Empire (1852 - 1870), under the rule of Louis-Napoleon Bonaparte, who was known ·as Napoleon III. The period is remembered as one of internal material prosperity during which industry and commerce flourished. Foreign policy, however, led the country into the disastrous Franco-Prussian War of 1870 - 1871. After the Paris Commune was overthrown on May 27, 1871, the Third Republic was established under the conservative Presidents Thiers and MacMahon. Subsequent attempts to restore the Bourbon monarchy failed, and the National Assembly voted a permanent constitution in 1875, which embodied a practical compromise between Republicans and Royalists. Time favored the former, however, and in 1879 the Republican majority of the National Assembly elected Jules Grévy President of the Republic.

Despite traumatic upheavals caused by General Boulanger's nationalist, revisionist party (1885 - 1889), the Panama financial scandal of 1888 - 1893, and the Dreyfus case (1894 - 1899), the Republic survived and a series of democratic reforms was initiated. Under Socialist pressure, labor legislation was adopted by the French Parliament. Foreign policy was marked by the conclusion of an alliance with Russia in 1894 and an *entente cordiale* with Great Britain, as well as by extensive colonial expansion.

France participated in the remarkable advances of industrial and technical economy at the end on the nineteenth century, but the country's geographical position in Europe remained its inherent weakness, all too tragically demonstrated by its emergence from World War I in 1918 victorious but extenuated.

At the time of Rostand's writing of *Cyrano of Bergerac* (1896 - 1897), France was applying itself assiduously to scientific research. At the same time, however, the country was not fully confident of its strength nor its potentialities; the occult and mystical sciences flourished; Naturalism was on the decline, and each writer, in accordance with his particular temperament, proffered his own theory about the latest *mal du siècle*. Society appeared to be more than bored; it was disillusioned. Nevertheless, both in the times and in the literature, a glimmer of hope could be seen, a hope that a writer would appear who would embody in his poetry idealism and mysticism.

In the overwhelming applause, then, that greeted *Cyrano of Bergerac* at its first performance on December 28, 1897, there was something more than admiration for a great theatrical work. There was gratitude for the poet who finally had dissipated the atmosphere of sadness and futility with which young Frenchmen had lived for so long. The sorrowful period of internal upheavals was coming to an end. Glory and the joy of action were once again realities and no longer illusory dreams. *Cyrano* marked a complete reaction against the Realism of the problem plays then in vogue. It was a new and fresh Romantic poem, with a folk hero (masterfully played by the great actor, Coquelin) whose identity was shared by all. Cyrano of Bergerac was the Frenchman's dream in action.

I *Family Lineage*

Not only Rostand's style but his entire being is "the man himself." So rather than relate the purely chronological details of his life, I have chosen to examine some of the diverse influences which molded his spirit and which are clearly reflected in all his dramatic works. His family lineage must be recalled, because the cult of the arts was in the family tradition. Eugène, his father, an eminent economist and member of the Academy of Moral and Political Sciences of Marseilles and of the Institut de France, was also a poet and translator of Catullus. Edmond's paternal uncle, Alexis, is well known in the world of music for his piano compositions, oratorios, and an opera, as well as a volume of critical and literary musical studies. A taste for music and consequently for rhythmic emotion and color is evident in Rostand's work.[1]

The writer's aunt, Victorine Rostand, should be be mentioned as the author of a volume of verse entitled *Violettes*. The family influence that perhaps gave Rostand's temperament its warmest colors, however, was that of his paternal grandmother, a beautiful and highly sensitive Spanish woman of Andalusian origin. From her, Edmond inherited his vivacity and his love for *le panache*.[2] In one of his poems, which appears in the collection *Les Musardises*, he writes:

> But my lyre . . . perhaps it is a defect?
> Is strung with the strings of a guitar:
> My grandmother came from Cadiz![3]

This drop of Spanish blood so colored his temperament that it actually constituted the strongest element of Rostand's personality. Hispanicism, according to one critic, is the need to see more than life in life, that is, the need to poeticize, the need to ennoble a gesture by endowing it with something fanciful yet noble and magnanimous.[4] A more ample, more meaningful, more beautiful, more poetic gesture is what Rostand sought, and which he defined as "the smile by which one excuses oneself for being sublime".[5]

II *School and Early Youth*

Born on April 1, 1868, Edmond spent his early childhood at the Thedenat School in Marseilles, a bright, luminous and bustling city, with its colorful crowds, its port and its ships, which easily aroused the young boy's imagination. He was an obedient and quietly intense child, very sensitive to the beauties of nature, and an avid reader who worshipped Walter Scott and Napoleon. His main diversion was a puppet theater that he built in his home with the aid of an old servant, and for which he constructed the stage sets and invented the costumes. After the Thedenat School, Rostand attended the Marseilles Lycée from 1878 to 1884, the period during which the Third Republic was establishing itself under the Constitution voted in 1875. During his secondary education, he proved to be an outstanding student, already revealing a deep sensitivity for literary studies, but unsure about his future career. The most memorable event during Edmond's lycée years was his consecration as "school poet," thanks to a translation into French verse of Catullus' poem to Lesbia's sparrow, which was highly praised by his professor. Rostand began publishing his first poems in 1884, in *Mireille*, a small Marseilles magazine.

Having finished his studies at the Marseilles Lycée in 1884, Rostand next spent two years at the Collège Stanislas in Paris under the auspices of his uncle, Alexis. The "little Marseillais," as he was called, was the best student in French composition, history, and philosophy classes. He was greatly influenced by and earned the affection of his professors, especially René Doumic, and Boris de Tanenberg, who introduced him to Shakespeare and Musset. Rostand's collegiate triumph was the publication of his essay on Molière's *The Misanthrope* in the Golden Book of the Collège Stanislas.

III *Early Writing and Marriage*

After his secondary studies, Edmond, installed in an attic apartment in Paris on the Rue de Bourgogne, began law studies in order to satisfy his father, who was concerned about his son's future. Edmond's aspirations were literary, while his father's were practical. In his dreary mansard room, after having fulfilled his duties to his father and his law professors, he would allow his mind to meander in a dream world of his own creation, and he made some attempts at writing drama: an unfinished tragedy in verse, *Yorick*, as well as two acts in prose, entitled *Les Petites Manies*, were the products of these early efforts. Rostand was dissatisfied with his work, however, and ascribed his inability to achieve an easy prose style to the fact that he was far away from his native South and that the Parisian climate was not conducive to flights of the imagination. He felt he could not find a "place in the sun" in a city where there was no sun and thereupon decided to enter the literary competition organized by the Marseilles Academy. His essay on the assigned topic, "Two Provençal Novelists: Honoré d'Urfé and Emile Zola," earned him the Academy's prize in 1887. Rostand's name became known to the general public, however, only in 1890, with the publication of his collection of poetry, *Les Musardises*, begun in 1888.

The term *musardises* is defined by Rostand himself in the preface of the collection as wasting time in idle chatter, loafing and prattling like children. He explains that under the cover of such a title, which implies extremely light poetry, it might be surprising to find some strains of sadness and melancholy, but the reason for this is that in the Walloon language *muzer* means "to be sad." And, finally, Rostand explains that a certain learned churchman derives the word etymologically from *Muse*, which makes it a logical choice for his poetry.[6] There is also a biographical element in Rostand's choice of the title: in his lycée days in Marseilles, whenever he seemed to be distracted, his third-year professor would say to him: "Mr. Rostand, you never know your lessons; you're always loafing [vous musardez tout le temps]."[7] *Les Musardises* are sweet daydreams and delightful meanderings of the imagination. They reflect the mood of a fanciful adolescent, a young man who searches for love and finds it, even though he knows that he is not destined to be a love poet. The verses are a pleasant and facile spinning of romantic themes, while his later collections, *The Canticle of the Wing* and *The Flight of the Marseillaise*, reveal his patriotic spirit. Despite a certain fascination, *Les Musardises* was not successful, and the critics gave Rostand no encouragement.

The year of the publication of *Les Musardises* also marked the poet's marriage to Rosemonde Gérard, to whom the collection is dedicated. Rosemonde was the granddaughter of one of Napoleon's marshals who fought gloriously in the battles of Wagram, Moscow, and Waterloo. An orphan, she was raised in a convent, loved literature, and composed poetry. Her book of verse, *Les Pipeaux* (1889), earned a special mention from the French Academy for the author's sensitivity. Rosemonde proved to be one of the happiest forces in the creative life of Rostand. She was the ideal companion for a poet, and a constant source of encouragement for him in the face of his failures, not least of which was the public reaction to *Les Musardises*. Even Rosemonde's godfather, the poet Leconte de Lisle, had forcefully suggested that Edmond should not have allowed his poetic fancy to run wild in the collection. When, in fact, the revised edition of *Les Musardises* appeared in 1911, the overly lyric and personal section entitled "The Beloved One" had been replaced by more sober poems.

IV *Days of Glory in the Theater*

Maurice, Edmond and Rosemonde's first child, was born in 1891 and seems to have resembled a portrait of the blond, curly-haired, sad-eyed Duke of Reichstadt which had hung in Rostand's bedroom many years earlier. The baby was named after one of his ancestors, and to the two Maurices was dedicated Rostand's drama, *The Eaglet* (1900), which treats the history of Napoleon II, Duke of

Reichstadt, whose entire brief life was spent in the Castle of Schoenbrunn in Vienna awaiting the opportune moment to return to France.

But it was *Cyrano of Bergerac*, written from April 1896 to January 1897, that marked Rostand's crowning glory. It was just at this time, too, that he risked his reputation as a playwright in the higher circles of influence by staunchly defending Dreyfus.

After writing *The Eaglet*, Rostand retired to Cambo, in the Pyrenees, in 1900, the year in which the Legion of Honor was bestowed on him. The pulmonary congestion that had begun to affect him during rehearsals for *The Eaglet* was temporarily arrested at Cambo, where he remained in close contact with nature and rare contact with friends—with the exception of Coquelin and Sarah Bernhardt. The following year, he was elected to the French Academy, but an unconscious feeling of exile persisted, at first instinctively because of his retiring nature and his illness, then also because he had achieved fame. He was timid in society, to which he had been exposed only lately and late in his life. He had always feared what he considered the greatest and cruelest form of human anguish: the anguish of success, the anguish of triumph. He had always cherished the loftiest concept of the role of the poet and of the theater, and now he felt that his responsibility was too great.

A deep sense of responsibility gave birth to the spirit of *Chanticleer*, that Rostandian spirit that had soared on the April evening of *Romantics* and that now began to decline, until it reached the dark, cold tragedy of *The Last Night of Don Juan* where the feeling of exile is experienced much more intimately and personally. Rostand's solitude at Cambo had inspired him to add something new to his poetic concepts: Nature. In it, he discovered a new world and a symbolic life. The deep significance of his retreat was the discovery of this new world in and around himself. The poet did not seek retirement in order to rest. On the contrary, he dedicated himself anew to his responsibilities and his duties. In *Chanticleer*, his last great work, there is a new note of idealism in a new realistic framework: the duty to work within the complexities of nature (i.e., the rooster's duty to crow in order for the sun to rise). Rostand worked ten years on *Chanticleer*. It was finally produced in February 1910 after various delays due to Rostand's ill health and the death of Coquelin, who had been cast for the principal role.

Despite Lucien Guitry's superb acting, *Chanticleer* met with a cold reception.

V *Declining Health and Success*

Returning to Cambo in 1910, Rostand complied with a request by the actor, Le Bargy, for a farewell piece at the Théâtre Français. *The Last Night of Don Juan* was the descending parabola for both the actor and the playwright. Whereas the symbols in *Chanticleer* had generally escaped the Parisian theatergoers who were unable to take seriously the actors costumed to represent roosters and hens, the Romantic symbolism of Don Juan was clearly felt by all.

France entered World War I in 1914 and Rostand, unable to fight as a soldier for his country, found himself thrust into another form of exile. This time, however, he did not withdraw. He plunged into the writing of vibrant, patriotic poems (*The Flight of the Marseillaise*) and visited the trenches in order to see with his own eyes the destruction, blood, and suffering that was devastating France. The horrors of battle undoubtedly affected him physically and mentally; the war years were his veritable Calvary. The armistice of November 11 brought an immediate sense of relief and exhilaration, but Rostand died about six weeks later, on December 22, 1918, without having given expression to his ardent patriotism in a play about Joan of Arc which he had dreamed of writing.

Edmond Rostand's entire life was characterized by an effort to rise to perfection and the superhuman. His love of solitude and dedication to simplicity were the other important facets of his character. He dreamed and cherished his ideals, which seemed to move ever farther and farther away from his grasp to the point of becoming inaccessible, but they nevertheless remained the guiding force of a lifetime. Edmond Rostand was a living illustration of the poet as a force in national life, a man of quality, and a teacher by example.

CHAPTER 2

Rostand's Poetry

ROSTAND'S collections of poetry reflect three definite periods in his life: his unperturbed childhood and adolescence (*Les Musardises*), his "classical" period (*The Canticle of the Wing*), and the war years with their accompanying hardship and horror (*The Flight of the Marseillaise*).

I Les Musardises

Composed during the years 1887 - 1893, *Les Musardises* opens with Edmond Rostand's word to the reader, giving him the dictionary definitions of the noun, *musardise*, and the verb, *musarder*, and warning him that the volume contains nothing but very light poetry—"bagatelles." The collection is divided into three parts: "La Chambre d'Etudiant" ("The Student's Room"), "Incertitudes" ("Uncertainties"), and "La Maison des Pyrénées" ("Home in the Pyrenees"). The poems in the first part describe the various elements in a student's life, ranging from his lamp, his couch, and the window of his room, to his classmates and his memorable school monitor, nicknamed "Pif Luisant." The second part expresses Rostand's unlimited poetic zeal on the one hand and, simultaneously, his doubts and perplexities in the face of the human psychological complexities which thwart the compelling desire to achieve perfection in poetry. The third part, imbued with a definite Spanish flavor, describes the Rostand vacation home in Cambo in the Pyrenees,[1] and the irresistible charms of nature.

In the first part ("The Student's Room"), the poems most worthy of note are the three dedicated to Pif Luisant, an ugly and grotesque figure to behold, but possessed of a beautiful and noble soul. Pif was the monitor at Rostand's school in Paris. Desperately poor, usually drunk, a vagabond by nature, Pif never succeeded in imposing discipline on the students, who instead made fun of him in their unkind caricatures. Pif was a poet, however, and the protector of the young, budding poet Edmond—which made them fast friends. Moreover, Pif openly defied standard society. He refused to conform, and in him Rostand found the symbol of his protest against all that is mediocre and vulgar. In the dreamer Pif, whose poetic language captivated the young Edmond, Rostand recognized his true master. It was Pif who "corrupted" Edmond by smuggling into the school the forbidden works of the Romantic poet Alfred de Musset, and by helping him write rebellious compositions against the Classicist Boileau.

In the first of the three poems dedicated to Pif Luisant, Rostand remembers him with much affection, and wonders whether the drunken derelict is still alive or whether death has relieved him of his constant thirst and cold. The second poem finds Pif still alive, reading Victor Hugo's verses on the doorstep of a tavern, looking thinner than ever but still very much in love with poetry and convinced that "our main duty is to sing for all." Pif's soul and imagination still soar, and Rostand still follows his mentor toward "l'azur." The third poem describes Pif Luisant's last days and his death—a victim of consumption. Edmond called on him frequently in his attic room, observing his beloved Pif's hands tremble more each day and his lips grow bluer. Pif tries to dissuade Edmond from becoming a poet, using his own example as discouragement. He tells his young follower that the poet is the victim of a serpent that destroys his "happiness"; that the poet is disdained, mocked, and scorned by society; that the true poet's bitter experience is not only to see himself rejected by humanity but to witness public (bourgeois) acclaim for facile, superficial, mediocre, and vulgar poetry. Even though glory may come to the "pure" poet after death, his destiny is to beg for a bit of recognition during his lifetime—only to be more despised by the masses. In his old age, the true poet, his strength drained and weary of the public's incomprehension, shamefully succumbs to the desire for glory during his lifetime: he renounces his search for pure poetry, and dreams of achieving the admiration of the bourgeoisie so that he may die content. The poet will compromise in order to obtain the comforts of life; he will stoop to mediocrity to obtain so-called "happiness." After beseeching Edmond not to dedicate himself to art, Pif re-

quests a last kiss. The only person to accompany his body to the
cemetery is Edmond Rostand, who has been dissuaded from the
vocation of a true poet by the tragic example of Pif Luisant; he is
now convinced tht he must become egoistic and strive for his personal "happiness." Just at the point of deciding to give up poetry
forever, a splash of exquisite nature arouses the poet in Rostand,
and he returns to his room to write his splendid verses on the death
of Pif Luisant.

Pif was a failure in life, but a source of inspiration to other poets.
The dedicatory poem which opens *Les Musardises* is, in fact,
Rostand's declaration of love for "les ratés" (failures in life), whom
the public scorns and insults because it cannot understand the
dreams and ideals of the great poet's struggle for beauty and perfection.[2] To all Bohemian artists, painters, musicians—the lost children
of society whose symphonies remain forever unfinished—Rostand
declares his fraternity and friendship, joining with the outcast
knights-errant to go out in search of Art.

Other poems of interest in "The Student's Room" are the triptych describing Edmond's attic apartment in the narrow, noisy Rue
de Bourgogne, his copper oil lamp, and his old red velvet couch.
The poems reveal the young student's intense solitude ("Je suis seul
à Paris"—"I am alone in Paris"), and his escapism ("Je rêve et
j'oublie"—"I daydream and forget"). Having come from the
luminous South of France, and keeping vividly and nostalgically in
mind the flower market of Marseilles, his dreary Paris room with its
heavy mahogany furniture, its worn velvet armchairs and cracked
ceilings, weighs heavily and hostilely on the poet's soul. Neither
love nor sun shines in his apartment. Looking out onto the courtyard, he sees only December all year 'round. His friend who comes
to visit arrives in a cheerful state of mind, but leaves with spirits
dampened by the atmosphere which stifles Rostand's poetic talent
and reinforces his belief that he will never be a great poet.

The room on the Rue de Bourgogne, despite its mournfulness, is
nevertheless a microcosm: in it live a poet, a mouse, and a flower.
The mouse's constant nibbling is the counterpart of the poet's
heartbeat; the rose's pervasive scent corresponds to the perfume of
his soul. The former fills the poet's ear with a repeated word of ad-
vice—"patience"; and the latter—"pride." These words give the
poet renewed hope, lessen his solitude, and even permit him to
laugh at the surrounding grayness.

The ode addressed to his oil lamp, personified and described as his only friend, stresses the poet's longing for warmth and affection. The lamp is associated with sleep:

> How many books I have read, how many verses written
> Under your humble lampshade . . .
> . . . when my eyelids were red with sleep![3]

The lamp also represents separation from the rest of the hostile world, expressed in a series of rapidly moving images which take the reader abruptly from the height of the attic room to the carriages rumbling through the sleeping street, from the blue-green sky outside the window to the passerby below who looks up at the lighted lamp. Close to his lamp, Edmond finds comfort, and the personification extends to the maternal protection offered by the lamp, whose flame slowly dies out—its own way of sending the sleepy boy to bed. In another vein, Edmond allies himself to his lamp in a vigorous battle: the struggle between thought and form, which gives rise to poetic creation. Then, continuing the personification, Edmond places a "hat" on the lamp's head: a cardboard shade that casts a golden circle of light on his desk. This is the arena for the forceful contest, the area into which the poet convokes all the dreams that are floating around his room. One by one, words fall on the battlefield at the foot of the copper oil lamp, in a sacred struggle "without arms and without cries." The fallen dead permit dreams to live—those poetic dreams which will be crowned by time for their valor in battle.

The third poem in the triptych evokes the old red couch underneath the student's window, on which he was wont to stretch out in order to concentrate his gaze on a square of silky blue sky. On this canvas, the sun makes its brilliant appearance; toward evening, the blue turns turquoise green, then black; the stars shine through. This is the firmament Rostand enjoyed contemplating for an entire day whenever he felt weary of life. On his couch, he could dream and forget. The minute he stood up, ugliness came into view: the asphalt courtyard, tubes, pipes, clotheslines, windows, walls, roofs—all the objects that intercepted his dreams. He recognizes, however, that it is "impossible to live without standing up," and the poem ends in the realization that one must be able to do both simultaneously: lie down to look up at beauty, and stand up to look at reality; see beauty despite ugliness, and in the midst of life's baseness never to lose sight of the pure silky sky.

The second part of *Les Musardises*, entitled "Uncertainties," contains a large number of poems revealing Rostand's introversion and melancholy. Inveighing against lethargy, insisting that we must *will* to be constantly active, the poet nevertheless falls occasionally into a state of boredom and passivity. An extremely beautiful morning troubles him; the purity of the air and the perfection of nature give rise to a feeling of the beyond, to thoughts of death, and Rostand succumbs to his melancholy. Another poem is written in praise of silence; still another evokes the delicacy, exoticism, luxuriousness and gaiety of "fêtes galantes" of the past, threatened by modern brutality, and the poem ends with Rostand's prediction that the human race is destined to a barbaric future.

Three poems in the section "Uncertainties" contain double-image constructions: "Les Deux Cavaliers" ("The Two Knights") is a dialogue between the Poet, victim of boredom, and his Soul; "Nos Rires" ("Our Laughter") is a variation on the theme of the mask and the face; and the third poem (untitled) juxtaposes Self and Conscience.

In "The Two Knights," the poet, plunged into melancholy, tormented by thoughts of death, and his heart "pierced with a knife [of boredom] as long as the nights," sends his soul five times to the top of the tower to see whether there is any sign of relief on the horizon. His soul reports back five times that there is nothing in sight except sordidness, mediocrity, banality, vulgarity, and vain discourse. The poet is convinced, however, that the day will come when his soul will perceive in the distance two knights approaching—symbols of strength—who unhesitatingly will enter the tower, take his boredom by surprise, and stab it in the back. What form the two knights will assume—Misfortune? Love?—is immaterial; the supreme certainty is that they will put the poet's *ennui* to death.

"Our Laughter" conveys the bitter sadness of the conflict between illusion and reality. Judging by the facility with which we laugh, says Rostand, we create an illusion of our own happiness and that of others. Superficial laughter is on our lips, but we avoid a meeting of the eyes, which go deep into the soul. If we really should look each other in the face, our laughter would perforce turn into sobs.

The untitled poem is an interesting dialogue between the Self and the Conscience on the subject of frankness and falsity. The Self is proud to declare that it has never stooped to feign, but the small, insidious voice of the Conscience murmurs that perhaps it is a question of laziness; perhaps extreme openness is not so desirable after all. Perhaps we need to learn to play a long role in life. . . .

On the theme of good and bad poetry, Rostand writes that a poem is like a rose, which needs time to prepare its perfume and blossom, in a slow process that cannot be hastened by the artificial methods of force used by florists. The poem entitled "Le Cauchemar" ("Nightmare") is a bitter denunciation of bad writers—an extremely well-constructed poem, vibrant with scorn and replete with onomatopoeia and repetitions expressive of the poet's horror at human abuse of printed words. The nightmare describes a group of prisoners in a cell with barred windows, looking out over the surrounding forest. The hard, cadenced sounds they hear are made by axes cutting down the trees in order to make paper to satisfy the insatiable thirst of writers, kings, tenors, bankers, tailors—and even poets—who are possessed of the urge to write. It is necessary to destroy nature to provide sufficient paper for all of them. The fact that nature itself provides poetic inspiration and that the forest shelters wildlife, perfumes the air, and offers shade and shelter is unimportant. The trees must be cut down so that priests, historians, women and children can all write their books. As the trees die and are transformed into printed pages, they are brought into the prison cell, which is nothing other than a library. As more and more books pour in, the prisoners inside the cell are gradually stifled and crushed between their backs. Pale and horrified, attempting in vain to escape, they cry out their love for the sweetness of nature and the beautiful world of the forest. Their cries go unheard, however, and the poem ends on a note of sheer anguish.

"Home in the Pyrenees," the third part of *Les Musardises*, takes us back to the poet's childhood, to the happy days spent at the family's vacation home in Cambo—a place of study, music, mystery, and love. Rostand was all the more attached to the region of the Pyrenees because of his grandmother's Spanish origins; in Cambo he can "hear Spain singing without leaving France." At the age of twenty, just as at the age of twelve, he feels the same anxiety to return to the irresistible charms of Cambo, which conjure up in

his mind innumerable allusions to Spanish influences on the French
literature he knows so well.

The most "Spanish" of the poems in "Home in the Pyrenees" is
"Le Contrebandier" ("The Smuggler"), a long, dramatic poem
composed during the poet's meanderings along the Spanish fron-
tier. After a picturesque description of the countryside, on the scene
appears a donkey laden with contraband metal objects of every size
and description. The bent old man leading the donkey is stopped by
the customs officer and refused permission to enter France. Turning
back toward Spain, unknowingly followed by the young poet, the
old man gradually straightens up and takes on a new, dignified
appearance. The poet is aware that he has seen this man before, and
finally he recognizes him: it is Don Quixote! Quickly, the poet
offers to wear the Spaniard's copper helmet (the famous barber's
bowl), and join Don Quixote in his idealistic wanderings. Don Quixote explains that he wants to cross the border because he feels that
"Europe is growing old" and has lost its sense of folly. His presence
would rejuvenate Latin blood abroad, which is growing thick with
age. To enter Europe, however, he must pass through France, and
France no longer loves him. France, which used to mock his wares
tenderly and lovingly, now is distrustful and has lost its sense of
humor. Sancho Panza has been allowed to cross the border (because
he bore no arms), and now he roams through Europe making a farce
of the legend of Don Quixote. Fired with enthusiasm for all that
Don Quixote represents, the poet, fearless and faithful, sets out to
face the perils of the smuggler's life, looking straight up at the blue
sky and wearing on his head a helmet that has now turned into
gold.

Rostand's deep, almost religious sensitivity to nature is best
revealed in this collection of poems. "Prière d'un matin bleu"
("Blue Morning Prayer") is the recitation of the phrases of the
Lord's Prayer by the elements of nature in turn: sky, earth, plants,
animals, insects, all of whom feel constrained to pray in Latin, so
beautiful and blue is the morning! Descriptions of honeysuckle,
broom with its showy yellow flowers, the song of birds, and twilight
in the Pyrenees charm the reader into association with the poet's
sensations—sensations which are best conveyed, perhaps, in a poem
entitled "La Fleur" ("The Flower"). Extremely well-constructed

and involving all the senses, the poetic image is that of not the traditional needle, but the flower in the haystack, whose stem pricks the ear of the lolling poet.

Another exceptionally well-conceived image is contained in the poem describing the branch of a weeping-willow tree, one leaf of which is captive in a babbling stream which flows below. Why has the leaf been taken prisoner by the water? Undoubtedly because it was eavesdropping, curious to know why the water was laughing. The other leaves on the willow branch think the leaf is undergoing harsh punishment, but in reality the captive leaf is proud and delighted to have been chosen to communicate with the vibrant stream.

Other poems use nature as the point of departure for philosophical or social reflections, such as "Le Mendiant Fleuri" ("The Flower-Bedecked Beggar"), a touching description of a nameless, faceless beggar, remembered only because he wears on his head a large mushroom cap with a phlox as a feather, thyme to lace his shoes, and lilacs and daffodils as patches for his torn clothing. The beggar's virtue lies in his refusal to show his ugliness, and the moral of the poem is that flowers planted in a dungheap are the most beautiful of all. Another poem describes a trained bear, forced to move from town to town putting on its grotesque act, performing for a harsh trainer and an even harsher public. The poem concludes with an expression of incomprehension as to "why this bear did not eat this man."

In "Tout d'un coup" ("Suddenly"), the poet describes the lights of a tiny village shining below the darkening shadows of the sky, and points out that, in the night, there is no difference between the lights shining through the window of a good man's or a bad man's home. The poem entitled "Les Boeufs" ("The Oxen") is highly reminiscent of Leconte de Lisle's well known poem, "Midi." The wisdom of the implacable, ruminating oxen is understood by the poet: unable to change their outward destiny, they find freedom in their inner dream. By extension, the wise man never takes his eyes off his dream, no matter what ills befall him.

"L'If" ("The Yew Tree") expresses metaphorically the yellowing of the leaves of an evergreen tree. The evergreen itself (purity) never changes the color of its leaves, but the surrounding trees (humans) shed their yellow leaves (calumny) onto the yew tree, attempting to stifle it, but the yew never changes its color underneath.

"La Brouette" ("The Wheelbarrow") is a very effective poem in the form of a parable. One cold winter day, Jesus and Peter return to earth. They encounter a peasant woman attempting to gather the sun's rays in her wheelbarrow. Peter makes fun of the woman, but Jesus, full of love and comprehension, approaches her and gently asks why she is out in the cold trying to gather sunbeams instead of dried wood and leaves to light a fire. The peasant woman explains that her dying child has asked her for the sun. Peter declares she is insane; Jesus muses that simpleminded people can work miracles of love. The credulous woman continues her act of faith, and the miracle occurs: the sun's beams accumulate within the four planks of her humble wheelbarrow, which now gives the appearance of being filled high with gold.

Two poems of extreme delicacy in "Home in the Pyrenees" are "L'Eau" ("Water") and "Ombres et Fumées" ("Shadows and Smoke"). The first (dated 1893) evokes the fountains of the town of Luchon, one of which may have inspired Rostand to write *The Woman of Samaria* in 1897. Water is described in all its forms and functions, in a series of personifications, alliterations, and onomatopoetic figures of increasing intensity. By way of contrast, in the second poem, Rostand identifies with vaporous, shadowy, uncertain things. He describes a variety of shapes, sizes, and forms of shadows and smoke, in a decrescendo of diminishing intensity, and concludes that the most appealing shadow of all is the unsubstantial shadow of smoke against a stark white wall.

Les Musardises contains a certain number of poems worthy of recommendation, especially those containing nature descriptions, but the collection falls far short of *The Canticle of the Wing*, published twenty years later.

II   The Canticle of the Wing

The Canticle of the Wing is Rostand's best collection of verses, and contains the poem that may be considered the key to his versification technique: "Les Mots" ("Words"), which will be discussed below. The collection comprises twenty-four poems, of which the first seven, reflecting the composite elements of the title, abound in personifications of song, winged images, expressions of flight, and a highly ethereal vocabulary. Most of the next twelve poems are dedicated to a strange variety of persons or groups, ranging from an empress to an entomologist. The collection ends with five long poems, including "Words" and "An Evening at Hernani."

The Canticle of the Wing" opens with the title poem—a call to all fearless men proudly to sing in praise of France's heroes. The Canticle (and all its variations—Hymn, Ode, Song, Chant) is the inspiration for humanity to set itself an ever-rising road to travel, parallel to the sun's rays. The Wing attaches itself to historical personifications—Century, Prowess, Exploit, Hero, Eagle, Lark—building up the poem in degrees of heroism. France's destiny, writes Rostand, is that its mothers will love their sons proudly, that its wounds will open toward the east (Germany), and that the nation must die for an ideal before it will rise again on wings of song. For Rostand, the inactive man is a weight on the shoulders of the world. We must all strive for the blue laurels of the ether, which are waiting on high to crown our heads. No one is unfit to fly, and the call of the wing is strong. Heroism, a reciprocal of love, turns crutches to wings and flesh to spirit. Even beasts of burden contain the seeds of wings. The last stanza of the poem proclaims glory to Prometheus, who courageously plans his flight while contemplating the wings of the vulture that is preying on his liver.

A series of sonnets continue the development of images in the sky: floating ashes of Rome's past glories, Pegasus, the star of Bethlehem, and the song of the French Cock raised to the sky, accompanying the flight of the Lark (Joan of Arc).

Of the poems addressed to particular persons or groups, the most notable ones are the sonnet to Sarah Bernhardt[4] (who played the title roles of *The Princess Far Away* in 1895 and *The Eaglet* in 1900), honoring her supremacy as a stage actress; and the ballad and sonnet dedicated to Coquelin (who co-starred with Sarah Bernhardt in *The Princess Far Away* and played the role of Cyrano in 1897), praising his stagecraft as well as his human qualities.

Of interest also is the poem to the students of the Collège Stanislas in Paris[5] (where Rostand had studied for two years, from 1884 - 1886), exhorting them to imitate Cyrano of Bergerac's beauty of soul, and even though their *panache* might not be visible, to strive to be swashbuckling in spirit.

Other poems in this section of the volume, less revealing of the poet's talent, are dedicated to Greek beauty and the resistance of its people—verses recited by the author from the stage of the Théâtre de la Renaissance on March 11, 1897, during the Greco-Turkish War; to the Empress of Russia; to Paul Krüger, the South African statesman who struggled against British domination; to Jean-Henri Fabre, the French entomologist; and to Gaston La Touche, a minor Romantic painter.

The five long poems concluding *The Canticle of the Wing* are far superior to the other poems in the collection, and offer the best examples of the poet's verbal alchemy. Rostand was in love with words, with each letter in each word. On them, he performed delicate vivisections to know and love them better. "Words," written in Cambo in 1905 and dedicated to his contemporary Jules Renard,[6] is a long poem divided into nine parts. The first three parts contain the image of a closet—a sort of Pandora's box—in which are locked all the words of all books that have ever been printed. An uprising takes place in the closet, and we hear the complaints and sobs of the personified words, who are suffering on the page where assassinations, massacres, and other cruel acts are described. Other words protest onomatopoetically against the dissecting saws that cut into their very roots, and the surgery being performed on them by the grammarians. Words have their own mind, however; they know they are everything and can do anything, so taking acrobatic initiative to render themselves energetic, elegant, leonine, or tragic, they join ranks to form stanzas. One wise old word, in the midst of the general upheaval, takes the floor to explain that words are living creatures that evolve like human beings. Although words may have twins, substitutes, or synonyms, there is a process of natural selection which assures survival of the fittest. The letter *h*, for example, is weak, and words such as *choeur* (*chorus*) risk mutations. The wise word explains further that words have their own vanity: they want to be printed by the best presses; the only order they wish imposed on them is by great poets; the only lessons they want to be given are the lessons of time. The fourth part of the poem dwells on the double esthetic of words: sight and sound. Words are beautiful on the printed page as well as falling from lips, and their two forms of beauty are inseparable. Verbal mystique lies in the fact that words may be read with the ear and heard with the eyes. The fifth part groups the "ugly duckling" words, who speak out to protest orthographic changes imposed on them, which mar their beauty. What greater ugliness than "paon," "héros," "libellule," "nymphe," and "bacchante"? The sixth part, on the other hand, groups words which demonstrate the imperturbable artistry of their composition: "glycine," "troubadour," "cygne," and "aumône" and "trône" with their graceful, winged accents. In the seventh and eight parts, language "reform" is protested by words who see themselves transformed into monsters and pygmies, and sense that their end is approaching; they would like to flee the printed page and literally become the beautiful things to which formerly they had only attached their names: air, roses, sky, evening, bees. . . . They desire to desert the pages of the classics as a form of respect to the masterpieces as they were originally conceived.

Modern tendencies which destroy beautiful words are condemned, and here Rostand uses an exceptionally felicitous image of the destruction of verbal Beauty: Venus being tattooed on the lovely curve of her shoulder. At this point, the poet begins to understand his nightmare of the closet: on this dark night of the uprising, the words are pushing against the barricades, seeking escape. Finally, the leather bindings of the books open, setting the words free, and the exodus begins. The last scene sees the poet waking from his nightmare, running to the closet, relieved to see that all his words are still there. The poem ends in an exalted declaration of love by Rostand for all French words, wherever they may be.

The second of the five long poems contained in *The Canticle of the Wing* is really a play divided into sixteen scenes, unfolding from 9:45 A.M. to 2 A.M.—a day in the life of the young lady, Sibylle-Anne Ogier de Mirmande, whose *précieuse* name is Doralise. The first line—a series of suspension points—indicates that Doralise is asleep. Following twenty-seven lines of beautiful description of nature emerging from the dark, "Doralise begins to awaken. She is awake." She goes to her window, under which the gallant Phylante, "marquis, musketeer and poet," is playing his lute; but she goes right back to bed, for noble ladies must not rise before 10 A.M. Lest the reader think Phylante and Doralise are in love, Rostand quickly disabuses him: both are playing a romantic game of love, and put-

ting on a highly refined act. Doralise really loves Tiridate, a knight-
ly alchemist; and Phylante really loves Garamantide, Doralise's
précieuse friend. Garamantide loves Phylante in turn, but pretends
to love Doralise's lover, Tiridate. A grandiose four-way feint, in
sum—four hearts secretly living a double lie! At this point in the
poem, Rostand seeks a rationale for all this feigning, and provides
two answers: (1) that love is a complex phenomenon, characterized
by mystery, secrets, and private agreements; and (2) that people
prefer to hear said about themselves what is *not* true.

It is impossible, however, to live a lie without feeling troubled,
and Doralise is indeed disturbed; she muses that by dint of playing
the game so well, she has to convince herself from time to time that
she really prefers Tiridate to Phylante. In her pretentious com-
positon of a portrait poem of herself dedicated to Tiridate, she finds
she has unconsciously tried to please Phylante even while declaring
her love for Tiridate.

Ten o'clock having sounded, Doralise may now rise according to
convention: a very exotic beverage of coriander and cinnamon for
breakfast is followed by preparations to receive her court of
flatterers around her bed. A typical session of *précieux* exchanges
ensues: perfect linguistic and table manners are debated; eating
jam with a fork is declared heretical. A rondeau on the subject of a
crystal seal sent to a forgetful lady is extemporaneously composed
by Tiridate; Phylante responds with an improvised burlesque
rondeau on the same subject, leaving the "court" with divided
opinions as to which poem deserves the prize. Doralise hopes
desperately that a polemic will arise which will make her retinue
famous; but an unexpected impromptu by a third poet, in the form
of an acrostic quatrain apotheosizing Doralise, settles the affair
without further ado.

Midday: an exquisitely served luncheon fails to tempt Doralise,
who is worried about the game of love, but she has no time to
ponder the problem since a coveted invitation to Madame de Rambouillet's court has just been brought to her. Summoning her maids
to begin dressing her for the occasion, she dreams about the two
men, and vacillates while making mental comparisons. She becomes
irritable with her maids, and seems unable to make up her mind
whether to wear a mask or a veil for disguise (but decides on the
former as more suited to the double-lie game). Finally Doralise is

ready for the outing: the first stop is at Arthénice manor, where, in a
bustle of beehive activity, the order and passengers of the carriages
are to be assigned. The other two ladies in Doralise's carriage are
her friend Garamantide and the singer Paulet, the beauty of whose
voice causes nightingales to die in despair, and three escorts. The
carriages drive through the towns and forest, while the passengers
make merry in true *précieux* fashion. Their destination is reached.
The celebration in Madame de Rambouillet's gardens is unforgettable, with music, dancers, Paulet's singing, liqueurs, and fireworks.
Doralise, keeping up the game, refuses Tiridate as her companion
for the evening. The trip back to Paris is enlivened by singing, but
Doralise's sleepy eyes are closed as she searches for a way to feign
that she is feigning love for Phylante, whom she has now decided
she really loves! The game of pretense has inevitably led to a real
attachment; this was Doralise's fatal destiny. At two o'clock in the
morning she falls asleep, but the reader knows she will wake up the
next morning to continue the sham. The extreme cleverness with
which Rostand has moved us along with the clock's hands, leaving
us with the feeling of a day vainly spent, is the overriding merit of
this poem.

"An Evening at Hernani," written in 1902 on the centenary of
Victor Hugo's birth, commemorates the famous author's best-
known drama, *Hernani* (1830). In 1902, Rostand visited the sleepy
Guipuzcoan village of Hernani, between Irun and Tolosa, to pay
homage to Victor Hugo and to identify himself with his cortege of
followers. Rostand has himself accompanied by an old Basque
shepherd, just for the pleasure of hearing the name of the village
pronounced with a Basque accent. With mild irony, Rostand points
out that the shepherd knows nothing of the illustriousness of the
village's name, but had it been the site of some famous battle rather
than the title of a drama in verse, he would have more reverence for
the spot. As it is, in the face of Rostand's visible trembling and emotion at the sound of "Hernani," the shepherd considers the man he
is escorting to be a bit mad. The poet, completely immersed in his
thoughts of Victor Hugo, notices the initials V. H. on the beret·of
the Basque village's municipal guard. He stops him to ask what the
initials stand for, and remains incredulous at the answer: "*Villa de
Hernani*"!

Continuing his thoughts of Hugo, Rostand muses that, when he left France for political reasons after Louis-Napoleon Bonaparte's December 2, 1851, coup d'etat, Hugo should have gone into exile here instead of the Channel Islands, for Hernani belongs to France more than to Spain. Rostand closes his eyes and in his imagination relives the young Hugo's trip to Spain at the age of ten, trying to recapture the gradual process by which Hugo absorbed Spain into his subconscious. He imagines Victor's mother, inside the carriage in which she was travelling with her three sons, pointing out the town of Hernani. Opening his eyes, Rostand enters the village church to pray to the mother of Jesus. Leaving the church, he prays to Victor Hugo, asking for the courage to continue writing verses in the shadow of the master who already has said practically everything so beautifully before him; he begs in his prayer for poetic inspiration, in the style of Victor Hugo. At the end of the poem, a passerby, with great national pride, points out the birthplace of Urbieta, the Spanish leader to whom the French king Francis I surrendered his sword. With even greater pride, Rostand answers that on the same street was born the French drama to which "El Cid"—Spain's national hero—could very well surrender his sword, in recognition of its superiority. Thus Rostand demonstrates his deep admiration for Hugo, as well as the sentimentalism and patriotism which permeate so much of his poetry.

"Le Bois Sacré" ("The Sacred Wood"), the fourth of the long poems, is a delightful blend of ancient mythology and modern technology. Breathing a new life into the Greek divinities in their various mythological activities, Rostand describes the gods joyfully dancing in the forest on Mount Olympus, when on the scene crashes an automobile! At the sight of the car, the gods' mirth is redoubled; but when the two passengers climb out of the stalled automobile, the laughter ceases: a young, modern couple in love stupefy the gods. The first to approach the car is Vulcan, with his natural instinct for iron. Jupiter, meanwhile, summons Morpheus to put the couple to sleep so that Vulcan can make his investigation untroubled, as the gods look on. Vulcan is absolutely enchanted by the fantastic machine; he caresses it, and finally disappears underneath it to enjoy the beauties of the car's grease, thus permitting the other gods—worse than customs officers—to go through the luggage inside the car. Each god finds something appealing: jewels, leather cases, tobaccos, perfumes, etc., from the best shops in Paris!

By mistake, Mars sounds the horn and Mercury uncorks a bottle of champagne, but the couple continues to sleep, so well has Morpheus done his job. All the gods become slightly tipsy on the Mumm extra dry; Venus wants to try the car, and proposes that Vulcan take them for a one-hour tour around Olympus. All climb in except Apollo, who remains faithful to his beautiful white horses. The car is ready to move, but one tire is flat and the headlights do not function. Jupiter summons Aeolus, god of the winds, to blow up the tire, and Psyche to provide light. In order to turn the car, Vulcan discovers that he has to go backwards, but ignorant of reverse shift, he asks Jupiter to summon Hercules, who arrives on the scene ready to perform his thirteenth labor. A push with his toe, however, suffices to turn the car around, and off go the gods. An hour later, the car is back in place, the couple awakens, and—miracle!—they find their automobile repaired. They resume their trip, even more in love because Venus has left some romantic traces in the car, and Cupid is a stowaway in the trunk. As the couple wonder who possibly could have pumped up the tire and restored the headlights, Cupid smiles to himself, lighting a gold-tipped cigarette.

The last of the poems in *The Canticle of the Wing* relates an amorous version of Hercules' twelve labors: the breaking of Omphale's twelve spindles, each one of an increasingly softer substance. The poem succeeds in conveying the sensuality, voluptuousness, beauty and craftiness of Omphale, as well as the breaking of the strength and resistance of Hercules, but lacks the grace and delicacy of the preceding poem, and probably is inferior artistically to Rostand's other poems on mythological subjects.

III   The Flight of the Marseillaise

The weakest of the three collections of Rostand's poetry, *The Flight of the Marseillaise*, was originally conceived as a single long poem, opening with the battle for Strasbourg and closing with the end of World War I. Rostand's poetic dream was not realized, however, owing to the physical and mental illnesses that affected him during the latter years of the war.

The various poems in the collection contain numerous personifications of La Marseillaise (France) which never seem to take flight because they are encumbered by a plethora of literary, mythological, and historic names and references. Bitterly protesting the war, firmly asserting Franco-German incommunicability, and deploring his own sense of despair, Rostand overreacts by singing France's praises too loudly. He sees the French army as saviors of the beehive that produces the world's honey; the burning of the beehives (war) is the work of the Teutons; the American flag is unable to fly for Germany, but trembles for France, and its sight gives courage to a personified La Marseillaise, exhausted from battle. Six thousand young women, prisoners of the Germans, join hands to sing "La Marseillaise" in defiance of the "enormous Beast with a musical instinct." "L'Etoile entre les Peupliers" ("The Star among the Poplars") is an exaggerated litany of catechismal praises to France. Idealizing young French soldiers, Rostand would crown all of their heads with laurels; he praises the Italian soldiers who died for Greece and France, and links Italy and France (the She-Wolf and the Eagle) in a strange and unlikely marriage.

On the positive side, *The Flight of the Marseillaise* must be appreciated for its poems in praise of action, for the expressions of Rostand's compassion for the families of soldiers missing in action, and his humanitarian reactions to the cold newspaper announcements of the horrors perpetrated during the years 1914 - 1918. He heaps shame on the coward and bestows nobility on the humblest foot soldier. The suffering of others becomes his own, and acts of courage fill him with justified pride.

On the whole, however, *The Flight of the Marseillaise* does not succeed in rising above mediocrity to the desired poetic heights, and the increasing irrelevancy of patriotism in our times has assigned it an unhappy destiny.

The chapters following are devoted exclusively to Rostand's dramatic works, without returning to his poetry, except for a few references in the concluding chapter of the book.

CHAPTER 3

The Early Dramatic Works

T HREE of Rostand's most significant plays were written
before the turn of the century, during the period that may be
characterized as the springtime of his productive life: *Romantics* in
1894, *The Princess Far Away* in 1895, and *The Woman of Samaria*
in 1897. The heroines in the three works are vividly portrayed, and
their stories form a triptych of Romantic love, ideal love, and
spiritual love.

I Romantics: *Youth on an April Evening*

Les Romanesques, rendered in English both as *Romantics*[1] and
The Romancers[2], is a comedy in three acts, written in an easy and
fascinating style, throughout which the youthfulness and joy of the
author appear constantly. A cleverly arranged surprise lies in store
for the end. It is not a *pièce à thèse* (a play that demonstrates a
theory) except in the sense that it sheds light on Rostand's poetic
ideas. The author skillfully presents the old, old story of two young
lovers who are strengthened in their determination to marry by the
opposition of their parents. The tale of Romeo and Juliet comes to
mind, as does the medieval legend of Aucassin and Nicolette. The
words pronounced by the love-stricken young hero, as the shadows
deepen and the sky grows bright with stars, closely resemble those
in the latter *chantefable:*

> Dear stars of heaven, high astral light,
> Millions on millions, blue and bright,
> Yet shall be put to shame this night,
> At high heaven's bars.
> She will appear. From your clear skies
> You suddenly shall see her eyes,
> And ye yourselves your rays despise,
> My poor, dimmed stars![3]

In the first act, two bourgeois fathers, Bergamin and Pasquinot, desiring to see their children, Percinet and Sylvette, united in marriage, but realizing at the same time than an arranged marriage would not be acceptable to two young, poetic-minded people, conceive a strategem in order to solve the problem: the two fathers feign mutual hatred and forbid their children to speak with each other. Naturally, the two young people meet each evening at the dividing wall between their fathers' property—certainly the same legendary old wall that separated the lovers Pyramus and Thisbe (the hero and heroine of a story by Ovid, later adapted by Shakespeare for *A Midsummer's Night Dream*), as well as the lovers in the medieval *Lai du Laustic* (*Lay of the Nightingale*) by Marie de France, who writes that the lovers' dwellings were juxtaposed and separated only by "un haut mur noirci de vetusté" ("an old wall blackened with age"). Percinet is seated at the top of the wall; on his knee is the book out of which he is reading from Shakespeare's *Romeo and Juliet* to Sylvette, who stands, attentively, listening at the bench on the other side of the wall.

The two fathers plot with a certain Straforel, a swaggering swordsman who plays the director in a feigned abduction scene. When night falls, Straforel and his men pretend to kidnap Sylvette to the music of violins in Pasquinot's private park. Percinet arrives on the scene, leaps to the wall, draws his sword, jumps down on the other side of the high wall, and engages four or five hired swordsmen in combat. They flee in the face of his prowess, and, as the violins play a dramatic tremolo as pre-ordered by Straforel, Percinet engages Straforel in a duel. The latter, after a few thrusts, puts his hand to his breast and falls, pretending to be mortally wounded. Sylvette is saved! Percinet turns to receive the blessings of the two fathers, who have arrived on the scene just in time to proclaim Percinet as Sylvette's savior, and to end their animosity in the marriage of their dear children.

In the second act, the wall has disappeared, but the harmony between the two families begins to dissipate in the face of the two fathers' idiosyncrasies. The hatred that previously was pretence is now assuming the shape of reality. The two young people are still in love, but a slight indiscretion suffices for Sylvette to learn the truth about the feigned abduction; and soon Percinet finds the exorbitant bill for services rendered by Straforel to the two fathers for his "first-class abduction" including charges for masks, dark mantles, torches, music, and a sedan chair. The lovers quarrel over this discovery. Angrily, Percinet leaves home, having decided to scandalize Don Juan himself by courting all the young girls in town.

The third act begins with the rebuilding of the previously demolished wall, symbolizing a return to the hostile *status quo ante*. The two fathers, however, are secretly seeking a reconciliation, because since Percinet left home, Sylvette has fallen into deep melancholy. Like Percinet, she too is searching for adventure and truth. She has just about decided to have herself abducted (this time without feint). Her kidnapper, however, will be none other than our good Straforel, disguised as Almaviva, who is still trying to obtain payment from the two fathers for his original bill by bringing the two lovers together again. Percinet, the prodigal son, fortuitously returns home at this point, having understood that he loves Sylvette more than anyone else. In the final reconciliation scene, Percinet confesses that they were both mad to have sought self-realization elsewhere than within themselves:

> See, poetry is in the hearts of lovers;
> Not in adventures only, nor for rovers.
>
> . . . .
>
> Poetry, love, but we were crazy, dear,
> To seek it elsewhere. It was always here![4]

The play is enchanting but at the same time disturbing. It fascinates and charms, yet leaves a feeling that there is something deeper in it than appears on the surface. Percinet, the young hero, whose head is full of Shakespeare, amuses himself by putting into verse, like Romeo, the story of his own love. He takes himself seriously; he believes that what he feels in his soul is immortal love. He is perfectly happy until the moment he is faced with the reality of Straforel's bill for services rendered. Then he cries out, sword in hand:

> I'm gone! I won't be treated like a child!
> I'll be avenged. I'm going to be wild!
> Romance, affairs, duels, so fast shall come,
> Don Juan, sir, shall turn over in this tomb!
> I'll kidnap actresses! I'll have my fill. . . .[5]

Percinet symbolizes sincere, proud youth, whose reality lies in the realm of the imagination; he loves all persons and all things because he has found an object to love, and then is unexpectedly wounded by the deceptions of ordinary, banal men. He is perfectly happy in the youthfulness of his poetic love, but after having caught a glimpse of a not-so-poetic reality which wounds his *amour-propre*, he becomes so impatient that, burning with desire to realize his hopes and aspirations, he is seized by a form of mad energy that drives him into town to seek debauchery. He returns home profoundly changed, for he has undoubtedly tasted of a more intense reality. There is infinitely more depth in his new poetic vision. It is still youthful, neither sad nor broken, but stronger and more passionate than ever because it has lived through an experience that has given him a glimpse of greater truths. Yet when Sylvette expresses regret at the passing of their illusory joy, Percinet maintains the reality of that joy, too, simply because they believed in its existence. The new vision, however, is poetry detached from the eternal *I*. It is beauty seen through a sad experience. The figure of Percinet is more a symbol than a character; in him may be traced the psychology of youth. He is youth personified, full of healthy and energetic joy. At the end of *Romantics*, he emerges more sober, having taken a giant step toward young adulthood.

As for Sylvette, she is just as enamored as Percinet, but frequently she behaves in a more practical manner. Freshly released from the convent, one of the first thoughts she expresses with confidence is that lovers' dreams are always realized, for she has read about them in hundreds of books. Later in the play, when Pasquinot is wondering aloud how he should approach the problem of telling Percinet the truth about the feigned abduction, she cries out (revealing a surprising amount of experience) that her father should not tell him anything, for men just do not understand certain things! Sylvette, too, seeks "adventure and truth" ("du roman et du vrai")—but within the confines of her garden. It is Straforel who opens her eyes to the "magic lantern" within herself, and so it is a new Sylvette that welcomes the return of the prodigal son. In Sylvette, too, character psychology is clearly traced, but at the same time there remains that disquieting feeling that forever marks a play revolving around the eternal struggle between illusion and reality.

The two bourgeois fathers, in their banality and solidity, are disposed to doing anything and everything to secure the happiness of their children. They suffer from very unromantic sicknesses (cold and gout) and very amusing obsessions in order to preserve the sense of dignity and self-respect befitting their white wigs. Completely devoid of youthful spirit and zeal, they never attain significant heights and are soon forgotten because they lack broader perspectives. They never soar on the wings of a Romantic, fervent poetry. On the contrary, they do not even understand poetry; nevertheless, they are good fathers who try desperately to understand poetry if only to be able to realize and satisfy their children's aspirations. It should be noted, incidentally, that the character of the two fathers never conveys that disquieting feeling that was noted in connection with the two young characters, Percinet and Sylvette.

Straforel amuses us by his manner and imagination. Listen to his tirade on the different types of abduction that he makes available for his clients:

> . . . .From a common ruction
> To the highest, sir. Imagine an abduction,
> Two men in black, vulgar kidnappers, creep
> Up in a cab. That kind comes very cheap.
> Next, night abductions. Those by day cost more.
> Pompous abduction with a coach and four,
> And lackeys curled and powdered.—Wigs, I figure,
> Are always extra — Eunuch, mute or negro,
> Sbirro, brigand, musquetaire,—in courses;
> There's post abductions, two horse; three, four horses,
> One can augment *ad libitum* the number;—
> Top-chaise abductions, always rather sombre;
> Abductions in a bag,—burlesque. Then take
> Romantic ones in boats.—Calls for a lake.
> Venetian gondola takes a lagoon!
> Abductions by the pale light of the moon!
> —Moonlight comes high, sirs, but it *is* good form.—
> Abduction sinister lit by a storm,
> Flashing of lightning and of steel,—quite grim,
> Mantals dark-hued, plumed hats with spreading brim;
> Abduction, country-style, one for the city;
> Torch-light abduction,—that one's rather pretty!
> The masked abduction, strictly classical;

> There's one to music, suited to a ball:
> The sedan-chair abduction makes a stir.
> That's gayest, newest, most distinguished, sir.[6]

In Straforel, we are actually making the acquaintance of the precursor of Cyrano of Bergerac and Flambeau in *The Eaglet*—two clever manipulators of words and swords.

Romantics, in sum, is a pleasant little comedy written in an elegant manner mainly to divert readers and spectators, but containing a moral also: we must have faith in what we are doing and we must remain faithful to love. The characters in the play, or rather the external stereotypes, are cleverly represented; the study of human psychology is well executed; the action of the play, however, lacks continuity. Toward the end it lags somewhat because of its over-abundant and contrived verbosity—a defect, incidentally, which will be found in all of Rostand's works. Some scenes are admirable, but they are isolated and scattered here and there throughout the play. The exquisite little tableaus, each of which depicts artistically and dramatically a particular mood or situation, do not derive logically one from another and have no continuity between them. The lack of logical connection from one scene to the next is what mars *Romantics* as a well-constructed comedy.

Rostand's language in the play, however, unreservedly arouses the listener's admiration. It is as fervent and unrestrained as youth itself. The plays on words, the rich rhymes, the unexpected assonances splash and tumble at every moment. Although the excessive refinement of the language lends a somewhat contrived and unnatural feeling, the total effect is one of verbal hypnosis, and this is the artist's intention.

Rostand's genius is revealed in his paintings of different moods, and in his large conception of life. His ideas are profound but simple. Rostand has given us a miniature study of life's poetry, but he has warned us not to take him too seriously. True love *will* triumph, but crafty fathers will nevertheless pull strings. The old wall is real, but it is also a mimic stage:

> At least, old wall, thy puppet stage, 'tis certain,
> Has fresh green branches festooned for a curtain,

> The park for centre, skyline for a frieze;
> For hidden orchestra, the April breeze;
> For properties, her blossoms every one;
> Shakespeare for prompter, and for lights, the sun!
> Like marionettes, on finger and on thumb,
> Our fathers made the actors go and come,
> But on that mimic stage this glory shines;
> 'Twas Love himself who spoke the puppets' lines![7]

The little rondeau at the end of the work captures perfectly the various poetic nuances of *Romantics:* happiness brings song to the heart; all nature and the arts chime in; and Love leads the orchestrated ensemble in a perpetual refrain:

> Dainty dresses and rippling rhymes,
> And Love, with flute and dart and bow. . . .
> Flowery foolishness, all five know. . . .
> Sudden tempests . . . but stilled betimes. . . .
> Ringing rowels and clanging chimes,
> A good, kind bravo abroad doth go. . . .
> Dainty dresses and rippling rhymes,
> And Love with a flute and dart and bow. . . .
> Home, a harbor from a hateful times;
> A little music, a scene Watteau,
> A pretty playlet, not long nor slow;
> Sires,—lovers,—a wall where sweet-brier climbs. . . .
> Dainty dresses and rippling rhymes.[8]

The curtain does not fall at the end of the play. Rostand's poetic instinct conceived that the "romancers" would disappear into the twilight, then into the moonlight, until the stage remained empty. The ending is unusual for the times, and serves to enhance the eternal quality of "Romantics."

II The Princess Far Away:
The Dream of a Medieval Knight Errant

Toward the end of the nineteenth century, the Parisian theatrical public was flocking to the performances of an admirable interpreter of the poets, an inspired actress, a queen of the theater who made tragedy and poetry come alive for the French—Sarah Bernhardt. To her, Edmond Rostand read *The Princess Far Away*, a play based on the "legend of the far-off princess." Joffroy Rudel, Prince of Blaye, the spiritual protagonist of the play, was a twelfth-century troubadour whose song about an *amor de lonh* (far-off love) is the origin of the legend. Some of the biography of Joffroy Rudel is known through a song written by one of his contemporaries, the troubadour Marcabrun, who sent the song "to Joffroy Rudel across the sea" after the latter had set off on the Second Crusade in 1147 with the Count of Tolosa, Alphonse VI, and his illegitimate son, Bertrand.[9]

Joffroy Rudel had known a free and easy existence but gradually became disillusioned with what life had to offer. He conceived of a love that could never bring disillusionment; the sensual man became a dreamer. After having participated in the Second Crusade with the Count of Tolosa and Bertrand, he met Eleanor of Aquitaine, queen of Louis VII of France and, after her divorce in 1152, of Henry II of England. Joffroy's liaison with Eleanor having ended in her deceiving him, he withdrew to his castle at Blaye where, with his friend Bertrand, he spent his time lost in dreams and composing bits of song. One day, some pilgrims from Antioch boasted of the beautiful and virtuous Princess Melissinde of Tripoli. Joffroy Rudel fell in love with her from afar; he dedicated his poems to her; and finally decided to join a Crusade to go to see her. Having fallen ill on board ship, he was brought to an inn in Tripoli, where Princess Melissinde went to visit him. He died in her arms, after which she entered a Carmelite convent.[10]

The plot of *The Princess Far Away* is constructed on the framework of a free interpretation of the legend, which embodies Rostand's predominant idea—the same idea contained in *Romantics*. The attraction in the twelfth-century legend lay in its seeming to answer the call of the Dream, the Ideal. It is far away and inaccessible, but efforts must be made to approach it. Joffroy Rudel, in search of his far-off princess, is Rostand in search of his Ideal.

The dramatist has adhered to the basic lines of the legend, attributed by some to Nostradamus. The character of Fra Trophimus was created by Rostand, and the story is highly idealized, especially with regard to the role of Melissinde. *The Princess Far Away*, like *Romantics*, is another glorification of idealistic poetry, but this time it is more serious and on a more sublime tone.

The tale is simple: a young poet, who is also a prince, hears some pilgrims who have just returned from the Holy Land speak of a beautiful princess of Tripoli. She, in turn, learns that the prince, Joffroy Rudel, is in love with her, but she is confined under lock and key to a castle guarded by the Chevalier in Emerald Mail, an emissary of the Byzantine Emporor, Emmanuel, whom she is destined to marry. Joffroy Rudel sets out on his ship to join her, but the entire crew falls sick with fever. Joffroy Rudel, in his zeal (once again, Rostand's own), exhorts them to continue the voyage. He fires their imagination with a vision of the princess; all the sailors aspire to see her; she becomes the Ideal Lady toward which each one rows. The fanciful dream gives them the impetus and the strength to reach their destination—the port of Tripoli—but the prince is close to death. He sends his friend, Bertrand, to the castle to fetch Melissinde and to bring her to him. Bertrand finally succeeds in entering the castle; he gazes upon the princess and falls instantly in love with her, without knowing who she is. Melissinde, too, falls in love with Bertrand, thinking he is Joffroy Rudel. Bertrand quickly disabuses her concerning his identity, but she persuades him to remain with her instead of going back to the ship. A din is heard outside: it is the townspeople announcing the approach of a ship with black sails. Bertrand thinks Joffroy Rudel has died, for this was the signal they had agreed upon. The black sails do not, however, announce Joffroy Rudel's death but rather the death of the Chevalier in Emerald Mail whom Bertrand had killed in order to gain entry to the castle. Melissinde, deploring her weakness in seeking gratification with Bertrand, decides to go to Joffroy Rudel, who awaits her with immutable love. She appears before him in all her splendor amidst music and flowers, and Joffroy Rudel dies in her arms at the height of his joy. Bertrand, following the orders of the princess, leaves on a Crusade; Melissinde withdraws to the Carmelite hill in Tripoli.

The plot is extremely simple and moves forward swiftly inasmuch as Rostand has observed the classical unities of time and action. From the point of view of the spectators, the most important figure in the play is Melissinde: she is Circes, Delilah, Omphale and Cleopatra all in one[11]—or, as Bertrand says, a "saint" and "at the same time a magician." She is beauty incarnate, presented in a splendidly sensual frame of flowers and perfumes. She is, however, prey to spiritual and neurotic crises intermingled with very modern subtleties. Nervously clasping her mantle, she addresses it as a weighty, destructive force:

> Mantle, embroidered, gemmed, thou crushest me
> With beryl, corindon, chalcedony,
> Jaspers and garnets from Assyria brought,
> With senseless pebbles, riches good for naught;
> O mantle, mass 'neath which I, pallid, bow,
> O sumptuous mantle, emblem fit art thou
> Of that still heavier weight, unseen of all,
> Which I must bear. . . .[12]

She will marry the Emperor in order to belong completely to her incorporeal lover to whom she owes her soul. On the other hand, she confesses that she owes him also her "taste for twilight" and that she is somewhat irritated by this far-away love. Her effort to seduce Bertrand is an almost sensual flirtation:

> I have dreamed of love sublime, not otherwise!
> If I forswear love mystic and sublime,
> Proudly at least I'll plunge in splendid crime![13]

She is a completely feminine figure who does not want her feelings to be "too specific," and we can hear echoes of Sylvette's melodramatic voice when Melissinde boasts of her readiness to commit the "great crime:"

> What woman doth not seek, if she but dare,
> To hold Orestes bounden as with chains,
> While his Pylades dies, he knows,—and he remains![14]

The character of Melissinde is not fixed, but evolving. After she is disabused concerning Bertrand's identity, she reaches an awareness and achieves a poetry of broader perspective. Her spiritual evolution is in a sense miraculous, thanks to the almost telepathic influence of Joffroy Rudel who is awaiting her in the throes of death. At the beginning of the play, she is in love with Joffroy Rudel, but her love is inspired by curiosity and vanity. When her physical attraction for Bertrand predominates in the third act, she deludes herself, and shutting fast all the windows of the castle, she refuses to admit "the silly fable" of "a white wing changing to a wing of sable,"[15] signifying Rudel's death. At the end of the play, Melissinde's spirit miraculously takes flight. She has one desire: to incarnate Joffroy Rudel's vision so that he may die happy and serene in the knowledge that his dream has been realized. No doubt Melissinde looks upon him with the sophistication of maternal eyes, for Joffroy Rudel is dying the peaceful death of a child.

Bertrand is the character who has made this spiritual evolution possible in the heroine—not through his transmittal of Joffroy Rudel's verses of poetry, but through his own infatuous love. Melissinde tasted of an inferior love (that of Bertrand), which made her forget momentarily the ideal love (that of Joffroy Rudel) that was awaiting her. Disillusioned by the ideal-less, dream-less love of Bertrand, or perhaps suddenly inspired by Joffroy Rudel's supernatural act of love, Melissinde reasserts with pride the superiority of her love for the man she has never seen:

> Did I alone dream only Love was king?
> The duty I denied rings like a bell!
> I come to thee! I come, Joffroy Rudel![16]

By way of contrast, Melissinde's maid of honor, Sorismonde, is made of baser stuff. She suggests that the princess go to Joffroy Rudel, so that he may die in peace, and then return to Bertrand and his love—an ingenious and perhaps charitable scheme in a certain sense, but scarcely one that might quench the thirst of a soul striving toward the absolute. Sorismonde represents the robust and crude voice of expediency; in her heart there is no inkling of Melissinde's delicacy and her higher, more noble sentiments. The difference between the two women is poetically rendered in a beautifully contrived contrast between the lily and the rose:

> SORISMONDE: Your lilies hem you in, your dreams redoubling.
> Lilies are pale and proud. Lilies are troubling.
> MELISSINDE : Perchance thou'rt right. Flowers foreign and afar,
> Can ye be false, who angels' sceptres are?
> With thyrses luminous as seraphim?
> Cloudy their perfume hangs, like incense dim.
> (*She lifts the sheaf of lilies and gazes at it.*)
> Perchance thou'rt right and these be evil flowers.

> I touch them, trembling, drawn by ghostly powers;
> Their lovely pride chills a more lonely one;
> And laughter loves red roses in the sun.[17]

Rostand underlines the opposition between the pale, mystic flower and amorous crimson in the treacherous love scene between Bertrand and the princess, for which the marble pavement "is strewn not with lilies but with red roses."

The character of Bertrand compared with that of Melissinde is considerably out of focus. He is, in fact, nothing but an obstacle in the princess' path—an obstacle that nevertheless renders her worthy of Joffroy Rudel's supreme love. He is a true friend to Rudel, so perhaps he deserves to escape condemnation. His lack of moral strength might be attributed to his lack of physical strength after so many heroic struggles. He has little ethical backbone, and none of Joffroy Rudel's strength of character. He is a strange troubadour, courageous and devoted, but a troubadour both in life and love. As he himself says:

> My heart is weak. It has no barriers grim.
> A hero passes and I follow him!
> Were I Provençal, were I troubadour,
> Seeing such love, if I did not adore?[18]

From Rostand's point of view, perhaps the most important character is Fra Trophimus, through whose words the author explains the moral of the story. Fra Trophimus' philosophy of life is that indifference is the supreme vice and enthusiasm the sole virtue. In an exchange on the ship's deck, his idealism triumphs over the pragmatism of Erasmus, the prince's physician. Fra Trophimus defends Joffroy Rudel's search for the princess as an exploit as noble and pleasing to the Lord as a Crusade:

FRA TROPHIMUS: For He gains all, or so I understand,
                By any deed disinterested, grand.
                Not less His own than the Crusade will prove,
                Or so I think, this beautiful, pure love.
ERASMUS: You'd liken then this rash adventure, sir,
                To rescue of the Holy Sepulchre?
FRA TROPHIMUS: Is His desire just that His tomb be free?

> Were that His very care, resistlessly
> He'd drive the infidel,—believe this thing,—
> Forth on the great sweep of an angel's wing.
> But no. He wanted to set free His own,
> Who lived, proud, idle, drowsy and alone,
> Selfish, lukewarm, the slaves of circumstances,
> And set them splendid, singing, midst the lances,
> Drunk with devotion, glad to die in deed,
> In self-forgetfulness, the soul's chief need!
> . . . .
> All true love's travail serves High Heaven's cause.[19]

The Princess Far Away is a simple story that relates the search for that which is essential in life. Some lines in the play are truly worthy of admiration, but the work as a whole contains the same defects of excessive verbosity and artificial melodrama that may be found in *Romantics*. Moreover, the literary and artistic value of *The Princess Far Away* falls short of the earlier play. Public reaction to the work was one of indifference, which forced Rostand into a twenty-month period of solitude, during which despair alternated with hope, until his personal emotion fell into harmony with a religious inspiration.

III   The Woman of Samaria:
An Historic Parable with a Religious Thrust

When Jesus heard that the Pharisees had found out that he was making and baptising more disciples than John—though it was in fact his disciples who baptised, not Jesus himself—he left Judea and went back to Galilee. This meant that he had to cross Samaria.

On the way he came to the Samaritan town called Sychar, near the land that Jacob gave to his son Joseph. Joseph's well is there and Jesus, tired by the journey, sat straight down by the well. It was about the sixth hour. When a Samaritan woman came to draw water, Jesus said to her, 'Give me a drink.' His disciples had gone into the town to buy food. The Samaritan woman said to him, 'What? You are a Jew and you ask me, a Samaritan, for a drink?' —Jews, in fact, do not associate with Samaritans. Jesus replied:

> 'If you only knew what God is offering
> and who it is that is saying to you:
> "Give me a drink",
> you would have been the one to ask,
> and he would have given you living water'.

'You have no bucket, sir,' she answered 'and the well is deep: how could you get this living water? Are you a greater man than our father Jacob who gave us this well and drank from it himself with his sons and his cattle?' Jesus replied:

> 'Whoever drinks this water
> will get thirsty again;
> but anyone who drinks the water that I shall give
> will never be thirsty again:
> the water that I shall give
> will turn into a spring inside him, welling up to eternal life'.

'Sir,' said the woman 'give me some of that water, so that I may never get thirsty and never have to come here again to draw water.' 'Go and call your husband' said Jesus to her 'and come back here.' The woman answered,'I have no husband'. He said to her, 'You are right to say, "I have no husband"; for although you have had five, the one you have now is not your husband. You spoke the truth there.' 'I see you are a prophet, sir' said the woman. 'Our fathers worshipped on this mountain, while you say that Jerusalem is the place where one ought to worship.' Jesus said:

> 'Believe me, woman, the hour is coming
> when you will worship the Father
> neither on this mountain nor in Jerusalem.
> You worship what you do not know;
> we worship what we do know;
> for salvation comes from the Jews.
> But the hour will come—in fact it is here already—
> when true worshippers will worship the Father in spirit and truth:
> that is the kind of worshipper
> the Father wants.
> God is spirit,
> and those who worship
> must worship in spirit and truth.

The woman said to him, 'I know that Messiah—that is, Christ—is coming, and when he comes he will tell us everything'. 'I who am speaking to you, said Jesus 'I am he.'
At this point his disciples returned, and were surprised to find him speaking to a woman, though none of them asked, 'What do you want from her?' or, 'Why are you talking to her?' The woman put down her water jar and hurried back to the town to tell the people, 'Come and see a man who has told me everything I ever did; I wonder if he is the Christ?' This brought people out of the town and they started walking towards him.

Meanwhile, the disciples were urging him, 'Rabbi, do have something to eat'; but he said, 'I have food to eat that you do not know about'. So the disciples asked one another, 'Has someone been bringing him food?' But Jesus said:

> 'My food
> is to do the will of the one who sent me,
> and to complete his work.
> Have you not got a saying:
> Four months and then the harvest?
> Well, I tell you:
> Look around you, look at the fields;
> already they are white, ready for harvest!
> Already the reaper is being paid his wages,
> already he is bringing in the grain for eternal life,
> and thus sower and reaper rejoice together.
> For here the proverb holds good:
> one sows, another reaps;
> I sent you to reap
> a harvest you had not worked for.
> Others worked for it;
> and you have come into the rewards of their trouble.'

Many Samaritans of that town had believed in him on the strength of the woman's testimony when she said, 'He told me all I have ever done', so, when the Samaritans came up to him, they begged him to stay with them. He stayed for two days, and when he spoke to them many more came to believe; and they said to the woman, 'Now we no longer believe because of what you told us; we have heard him ourselves and we know that he really is the saviour of the world'.

John, 4

With the intention of writing a Biblical drama for Holy Week, Rostand turned his attention to the Fourth Gospel according to Saint John. *The Woman of Samaria*, an "evangel in three parts," is simultaneously the weakest and the best of the playwright's early works, because as a dramatic work it contains all the weaknesses and defects of composition which have been pointed out in the other early plays, but as a gospel in painting it is a composition worthy of admiration. *The Woman of Samaria* is an artistic study of the soul.

The play is composed of three tableaus: "Jacob's Well," "The Gate of Sichem," and "Salvator Mundi." The first tableau is set against a Biblical backdrop of fig and olive trees, pines, cypresses,

the blue valley of Sichem, and Mounts Ebal and Gerizim. It is a sort
of prologue divided into two scenes. First, there is the appearance
of the patriarchs of the Old Testament: Abraham, Isaac, and Jacob,
who prophesy that God has chosen that beautiful spot, Jacob's well,
to perform a great miracle. Built on a series of rapid rhymes of oc-
tosyllabic verses, the scene is a sort of religious dance executed by
the illustrious patriarchal shades who then disappear into the morning light. Next, the people of Samaria arrive on the scene, bemoan-
ing the spiritual darkness in which they grope, and discussing the
probability of the arrival of the Messiah. Jesus appears, followed by
his apostles. Because they are Jews, they are received with hostility
by the Samaritans—a people blinded by self-seeking and greed.
The apostles curse them, but Jesus relates to them the parable of the
Good Samaritan. The crowd disperses and goes in search of food.
Thereupon Photine, the Woman of Samaria, appears, her amphora
on her shoulder, expressing her voluptuousness in suggestive song
which Rostand adapted from the Biblical *Song of Songs*. Christ
reveals his identity to Photine in a scene that invariably arouses
deep emotion in the spectators. Photine utters the very words that
Jesus has longed to hear: "I think he comes to teach us everything."
He bids her to lift her head and behold her soul's desire. Photine
sinks to her knees, then suddenly bursts into song—the same bold
love song that accompanied her first appearance on the scene. She
stops short, aware of the sacrilege, but Jesus bids her to feel no
shame, for he has received her song—the only words she knows how
to sing—as a sweet gift of prayer. Rich in poetry, this is perhaps the
best scene in the play and the one which is most expressive of the
author's thought.

The curtain rises on the second tableau—a marketplace. The
apostles are unable to buy food because the vendors consider them
enemies and refuse to deal with them. In the background, the old
folk gossip about the strumpet, Photine, whom they wish to banish
from the village because of her dissolute life. Photine enters. Filled
with fervor for the Lord, she attempts to convince the townspeople
that the Messiah is among them. The merchants around her continue hawking their spices, necklaces, pigeons, and sparrows, while
others treat her as a madwoman. The priests appear on the scene;
Christ miraculously allows the illiterate Photine to quote the Scrip-

tures to them. Thanks to her magnificently lyrical rhetoric, she finally succeeds in urging the crowd to Jacob's well, as the merchants mutter bitterly that she is hurting their trade.

The third tableau contains the sweep of an immortal gesture and is a sort of apotheosis of Christ. It is inferior to the second tableau, however, despite its considerable movement and local color. It is simply a picture of Christ receiving homage from Photine and the people of Samaria. The recitation by Jesus of the prayer, *Our Father,* repeated after him by Photine, concludes the play—an ending that joins divine inspiration and human life.

Such is the entire plot of *The Woman of Samaria.* With the exception of the second tableau, which is a small dramatic masterpiece in itself, there is practically no action, but no action is needed, of course, in a painting. Rostand's depiction of life, and especially of life and thought during the time of Christ, is plausible, and the characters of the apostles are well delineated. Nonetheless, the central interest of the play lies in the character of Photine, whose part was written for Sarah Bernhardt.

A beautiful courtesan, gay and dissolute, Photine first appears on the scene singing a bold love song. She ultimately becomes a saint, following a transformation which is unexpected as much as it is miraculous. Before her encounter with Jesus, she never entertained any serious thoughts; a harlot, she lived only for pleasure. The words of the Messiah arouse her curiosity, but only because the Messiah is handsome! Through a miracle, however, Jesus reveals the truth to her; immediately the courtesan's quest for sensual pleasure ends and her thirst for love is slaked. She expresses the emptiness and dissatisfactions of her past experiences, contrasted with the thirst-quenching love for Christ, in figures of speech appropriately related to water, the well, pitcher, cistern, dew, spring, flood, etc.

> I thirst no more, who was devoured with thirst!
> I sought the broken cisterns every one.
> I drank,—and thirsted ere the draught was done!
> Sometimes I thought I loved. To love, I knew,
> Would slake my thirst. That love was never true.
> It left me parched and dry,—a tortured thing.
> Someone would tell me of another spring.

> Hope of new cisterns sunk in newer lands
> Drove me, my empty pitcher in my hands.
> . . . .
> With the old gesture, though my soul would tire,
> I lowered the empty cruise of my desire;
> Always I found the same deceitful thing,—
> Roiled, brackish waters from a troubled spring.
> From my hot lips the faithless pitcher fell.
> Always my cruise was broken at the well!
> . . . .
> And now my soul seems bathed with morning dew.
> Out of my shadows I have caught the gleam,
> The rainbow arc above the living stream.
> . . . .
> Sing, Living Water. Cast upon my soul
> And all its dust, the flood that makes me whole![20]

In the second tableau, Photine's zeal conquers the hearts of the
Samaritan people. At first, she is greeted with disdain and threats,
but after having made a public confession as a token of her sincerity, she is transported by her own eloquent fervor above and beyond
the indifference, the selfishness and the doubt of the townspeople.
This struggle is truly dramatic; the feeling that Jesus lives within
her is overwhelming. In the presence of the Lord, however, Photine
is no longer the great Samaritan prophetess but simply a sinner
purified by love. Nevertheless, she remains the central figure
throughout the play, and from her lips come the most celebrated
words of the Lord.

Perhaps the inherent defect of the play is the fact that the figure
of Christ does not lend itself easily to the character of a dramatic,
theatrical hero. He does not act; he remains seated during the two
tableaus, and although he undoubtedly represents the spirit of
divine tranquillity, he does not come through either as the Son of
Man nor as the Son of God. The people of Samaria expect the
Messiah's appearance in the form of "a warrior," "a priest," "riding
upon the clouds," "some fabled beast," "strong and joyous," "weak
and wan." He appears as none of these. Christ is very much a man.
Throughout the work there is even a slightly irreverent flavor: the
Lord's words, for example, are infused with the cult of the
beautiful:

> Conforming to the graceful urns they bear,
> Their bodies, slender vases; handle-wise
> Their curved arms lifted to the brooding skies.[21]

The cult of the beautiful seems to be almost identified with Truth and Beauty themselves. Christ declares himself ready to prostrate himself before Photine—the courtesan—who reminds him of his mother! He champions terrestrial love as paving the way toward celestial love. He says, in fact: "The love of Me comes always to a heart / Where lesser, human loves have had a part."[22]

The language and style of the play are too refined and, once again, too affected. One example will suffice:

> The sweetness ye find in a draught from this cruise
> Comes not from lilies the distillers bruise,
> Nor honey-comb all golden-sweet.[23]

Such exaggerated style contrasts too strongly with the simple and sublime greatness of the story. Moreover, Rostand seems unable to suppress his love of the spectacular in the form of parades: one was already witnessed in the last act of *The Princess Far Away*, and in *The Woman of Samaria* another procession: the arrival on the scene of the Samaritan people, heralded by Photine's appearance at the top of the hill, breathless, dishevelled, her arms full of flowers, her eyes splendid. She is preceded by a crowd of excited children who tumble recklessly down the footpath, waving olive branches. She is followed by a throng that rushes to throw itself upon Jesus. The scene is much inferior to Melissinde's arrival at the inn of Tripoli in the earlier play, but undoubtedly has stage value.

Rostand is a master of abrupt changes of gesture or sentiment in his characters. Accordingly, "miracles" are introduced into this play in an artistic and natural way, but somehow they are not manifestations of a divine intervention because they occur in too rapid succession, especially in the closing scene of the play, and thereby resemble too closely the rapid, ordinary changes in the other works—notably, *Cyrano of Bergerac*. The "miracles" in *The Woman of Samaria* are only brilliantly dramatic gestures—significant, certainly, but they might have been much more so. The absence of a truly mystic sense is manifest in the two little scenes that strike the artistic sense negatively by their boldness: the scene in which Photine offers her song of earthly love in homage to Christ who accepts it; and the episode in which Rostand puts into verse the simple and sacrosanct words of the Bible. If the playwright had paraphrased, or if he had allowed Photine to sing licentious songs, he might have succeeded, but by mixing the audacious songs of a courtesan with the divine expression of a prayer, the effect is slightly shocking and somehow reveals a certain lack of taste.

Rostand loves those who "have not succeeded"—those to whom he had dedicated *Les Musardises*. In *The Woman of Samaria*, we meet them for the first time. When Photine says to the Lord that the crowd awaits him, he cries out his thanks to God the Father for having sent him among the humblest of his creatures. Likewise, when Photine is about to reach the city, she says:

> But He delighteth humble souls to lift,
> Loves the unlovely, quenches bitterest thirst,
> —This gracious Lord,—and blesses the accurst,
> Pities the helpless, looks upon the least,
> Loves the poor man, the child, the bird, the beast—
> The small, sad donkey,—wistful dogs we beat,
> And publicans . . . and women of the street.[24]

Although there are many beautiful elements in *The Woman of Samaria* and it is clearly the work of a sincere artist and an inspired genius, the play's inspiration is solely poetic and dedicated to the cult of physical beauty. Rostand succeeded in transmitting the tranquil majesty of the Biblical poems and in giving us the impression of quiet harmony—a state of mind rare for him. Photine's eloquence is often of a simplicity that touches on the sublime. As for the thesis of the play, it is of the simplest: "One must sacrifice one's life to one's ideal." Edmond Rostand sought inspiration in the Bible in a moment of disillusionment. When mankind seemed to him to be vain and deceitful, he made a spiritual retreat and turned toward the Holy Scriptures. In the end, however, what is the message of the play? Is it Christianity pure and simple? It is not the splendid and eloquent Christianity of Bossuet, nor the supernatural and artistic Christianity of Chateaubriand, nor the vast, vague Christianity of Renan. Rostand's Christianity does not resemble that of these three great writers, because there is really nothing splendid, super-natural, artistic, nor vague in it. It is a splendidly affected Christianity, as artistically simulated as the cult of the beautiful. Rostand knows his Bible well; he knows the spirit of his times well; but he has no doctrines. Here lies the great defect of the work: it does not contain a philosophy; it is a sentiment, a gesture, a pale reflection of his taste for *panache*. Rostand's Christianity, in sum, differs from that of Christ, because the former is terrestrial, whereas the essential quality of the latter is supernatural.

Another period of solitude followed *The Woman of Samaria*, from which Rostand emerged with a new poetic direction. An intensification of pride and independence filled his spirit; he was to clothe a dream of glory, talent, and national pride in the costume of Cyrano of Bergerac, and pour into that Frenchman's soul Rostand's own cult of the ideal, love of sacrifice, self-denial, and heroic virtue.

CHAPTER 4

The Masterpieces

THE two plays that may be characterized as Rostand's most developed and mature works—*Cyrano of Bergerac* and *The Eaglet*—were produced in 1897 and 1900, respectively. The former is the glorious burst of the summer of Rostand's life. The latter was written at the beginning of a painful period of illness, destined to become the author's melancholy autumn.

I   Cyrano of Bergerac: *A Dream in Action*

In about three and a half centuries of modern theatrical history, there have been recorded in France only two other triumphs comparable to that of Rostand's *Cyrano of Bergerac:* the first was Corneille's *Le Cid*, produced in 1637 during the time of Richelieu; the other, *Le Mariage de Figaro* by Beaumarchais, presented in 1784 in the dawn of the French Revolution.

Cyrano of Bergerac was first produced on December 28, 1897, at the Porte Saint-Martin Theater. Exactly one hour after the curtain had fallen, practically the entire audience was still in the theater applauding. The most curious historic aspect accompanying the play's production was the pessimism that had marked the preparations and rehearsals. Even though the name of Edmond Rostand was well known in turn-of-the-century Paris, the idea of an heroic-comic drama in rhymed alexandrine verse, built on an historic background in the Romantic manner of sixty years earlier, constituted an anachronism. The Parisian public was sophisticated and demanding, but at the same time seemed to be avid for nothing but Imperial plays and easy *pochades* (light comedies).

The Fleury brothers, who were the directors of the Porte Saint-Martin Theater, after having accepted *Cyrano of Bergerac* for production, regretted it almost immediately afterward. They were pessimistic about its success and felt that if the play ran for a dozen performances, it would be a stroke of luck. In the face of such a negative attitude, it was decided to hold production expenses down to a minimum. Rostand found himself in the predicament of having to pay for the actors' seventeenth-century costumes—in the amount of one hundred thousand francs—out of his own pocket. As for the stage sets, they were so meager that during the dress rehearsal Rostand broke down and was on the verge of assaulting the stage designer. Notwithstanding the famous Constant Coquelin's zeal for the part of the protagonist which was his, pessimism prevailed throughout the theater. One of the members of the company asked Coquelin what his predictions were regarding the play's success; he answered in a single word, shaking his head negatively: "Dark." Instead, that night of December was to mark the beginning of a glorious career on stages throughout the world for the swashbuckling swordsman-poet, Cyrano of Bergerac. Capricious and unpredictable in its reactions, the Parisian theatrical public had nonetheless been able to discern accents of an authentic poetry behind the verbal virtuosity and the visual artifices of the play.

The story of Cyrano is well known in its broad lines. As told by Edmond Rostand, it reveals an ingenuousness and, in many verses, a quixoticism recalling the author's Spanish ancestry. Cyrano is an unvanquished swordsman and an affected, versatile poet, possessed of an enormous, grotesque nose which "arrives so long ahead of him" that it prevents him from giving free rein to his true nature, that of an incurable sentimentalist. He is secretly enamored of his beautiful cousin, Roxane, who in turn loves the young soldier, Christian de Neuvillette, an attractive man but completely devoid of poetry and wit. Roxane, fearful that the gentle Christian, who has just joined the corps of Gascon cadets, will suffer in the hands of his rough and rude fellow soldiers, entrusts him to her cousin, Cyrano. The latter takes his assignment so seriously and conscientiously that he even composes for Christian highly perfected love letters for his beautiful lady. In fact (in one of the most famous scenes of the play), taking advantage of the darkness, he boldly and passionately declares his love to Roxane, who is on the balcony of her home. Cyrano then altruistically withdraws to allow Christian to receive Roxane's kiss. In the meantime, however, the Count de Guiche, commander of the cadets, has also fallen in love with the beautiful Roxane. Unable to stop the marriage of the enamored young couple, he takes his vengeance by sending Christian and Cyrano to besiege the town of Arras. During the siege, Cyrano's passionate correspondence grows more voluminous, and his letters begin to produce a profound change in Roxane, rendering her love deeper and more spiritual. Now she loves Christian no longer for his external beauty but for his soul—that is, she loves Cyrano. Suddenly and unexpectedly, she appears at the Arras military camp, but on that very day, Christian, who now understands that Roxane has unknowingly fallen in love with Cyrano, has decided to tell her the truth about the correspondence. Realizing he is loved for someone else's spirit and intelligence, he voluntarily seeks his death; he is wounded in battle and dies.[1] Cyrano, out of respect for his friend, keeps the secret for fifteen years. On the verge of death resulting from a long illness caused by a falling beam striking his head, Cyrano, in delirium, confesses his long, immutable and unrequited love to the anguished Roxane. Dying, he lifts his sword high, and his last noble, proud words are: "Stainless, unbent, I have kept . . . / . . . My plume! *mon panache*"[2]

Such is the story that, bursting forth in sonorous verses and in a kaleidoscope of glistening images, has been holding audiences enthralled for almost eighty years. The student who recently declared that, in this age of cosmetic surgery, Cyrano of Bergerac is no longer plausible nor relevant, has, of course, missed the whole point of the play. It is not Cyrano's nose that prevents Roxane from loving him; it is rather the fact that he is not Christian. Even if Cyrano had been endowed with a beautiful nose, Roxane would still not love her cousin. The existence of the handsome Christian, speaking and writing with beauty borrowed from Cyrano's soul, is the image that holds Roxane enthralled, and her "pink lip will inevitably tend toward his blond moustache."[3] Roxane does not find Cyrano ugly, but a normal-nosed Cyrano would not satisfy her esthetically either.

And yet the nose is what has immortalized Rostand's character. Famous actors—Constant Coquelin, Ralph Richardson, José Ferrer, Gino Cervi, Jean Piat, Christopher Plummer—their faces disfigured by an enormous false nose, have been acclaimed and will be remembered for their interpretations of Cyrano of Bergerac. In

North America, the character was made familiar through the adaptations and stagings of Walter Hampden and Anthony Burgess. Such an abundance and variety of interpretations of the character of Cyrano suggest that part of this study should concern itself with the figure of the real Cyrano, since Rostand's point of departure for the play was the character of an authentic personage who lived in Paris in the seventeenth century during the time of Richelieu and Mazarin.

Before focusing on the real Cyrano, however, it may be of interest to note that as a young boarder at school, Edmond Rostand, already distinguished among his companions for his talent in composition, had offered to write love letters and poems for a friend of his, who copied them over and sent them to his young girlfriend. This personal recollection somehow imposes itself on the chronicles that have created the immortal trio of Cyrano, Christian, and Roxane. Moreover, Rostand's wife, in her book about her husband, relates an anecdote that sheds light on how the first idea came to the dramatist for the writing of *Cyrano of Bergerac*. Rosemonde states that Edmond was spending a summer in the town of Luchon, a resort in the Haute-Garonne, where he happened to meet, beside a fountain, a young man who obviously had been grievously disappointed in love and was nursing his sorrow. Edmond drew out the boy's story, then spoke to him at length, consolingly and paternally. For several days, Amédée returned to the fountain to listen to Edmond's "teachings," after which he disappeared. Rostand was quite triumphant when, some time later, he met the young lady involved and she said to him in a burst of passion: "You know, my little Amédée, whom I had judged to be so mediocre, is marvelous: he's a scholar, a thinker, a poet . . .". Amédée was, of course, none of these things; he was just a pale reflection of her ideal, but the idea for *Cyrano* was born.[4]

When Rostand submitted his manuscript of *Cyrano of Bergerac* for publication, he inscribed on the first page:

It is to the soul of CYRANO that I wished to dedicate this poem. But since it has entered into you, COQUELIN, it is to you that I dedicate it.[5]

Coquelin, as has been noted already, was the first actor to portray the role of the poetic swordsman with the long nose. In the light of

Rostand's dedication, it is reasonable to ask how much of the soul of the real Cyrano passed on to the stage, and how much from the stage into the legend; or, better yet, to ask why Rostand's imagination was so fired by the figure of a Gascon cadet who died at the age of thirty-six in the most melancholy obscurity.

The first encounter with the real, historic Cyrano is slightly disappointing: the Gascon cadet was, in fact, not a Gascon, even though he served in the company which subsequently became legendary. Savinien de Cyrano (the name given to our hero at the baptismal font) was born in Paris, of Parisian parents, on March 6, 1619, in one of the oldest and most populous neighborhoods of the capital—Les Halles. The family was rather well off, and enjoyed the prestige of a modest title of nobility. His father's name was Abel de Cyrano; the noble particule, de Bergerac, appeared later, following the acquisition of a castle on the outskirts of Paris. There were, in reality, two castles. The first, Mauvières, still exists today, although much transformed by restorations over the last century. The second castle has disappeared; not even its ruins remain. It is known, however, to have been called Bergerac, and was located near the village of the same name (now called Sous-Forêt) in the Chevreuse valley. According to established usage of the time among noble families, Abel's first child, Denyse, was authorized to use the name Cyrano de Mauvières; the second, Savinien, future swordsman and poet, Cyrano de Bergerac. It was probably the suffix -ac that misled Rostand and prompted him to make his hero a Gascon gentleman. Names of families and villages ending in -ac are, in fact, typical of Gascony. It is possible, too, that the original owners of the castle and fief were Gascons.

In accordance with the practices of the time, male offspring were sent to board with churchmen, and female offspring to convents. Savinien was no exception. His early education at Mauvières was entrusted to a country priest, who also had charge of Cyrano's future friend and apologist, the pious Henry Le Bret. At the age of twelve, after five years of what the great Italian dramatist, Count Vittorio Alfieri, a century later, would have defined as "ineducation," Cyrano left the boarding school. He had won a scholarship for the Collège de Beauvais in Paris, where he remained for six years and learned to detest tradition, cultural Aristotelianism, and the constituted authorities which were the mainstays of seventeenth-century society.

At this point in his life appeared the beautiful lady who was destined to become the inspiration for Roxane. In Rostand's play, her name is Madeleine Robin, and she is in love with the handsome Christian de Neuvillette. The real Cyrano de Bergerac did indeed have a cousin with a not dissimilar name: Madeleine Robineau, bourgeoise by birth, but married to a nobleman, the Baron de Neuvillette. Through her marriage in 1635 she had become a member of Parisian high society and stood out conspicuously among the most highly considered ladies. It was she who took charge of Cyrano's social education. It is not known whether the Baroness de Neuvillette was really a *précieuse* like Rostand's Roxane, but it is known that she had two great passions—good food and dancing—and that, like Roxane, she was noted for her "peach complexion." It was in her company that Cyrano learned the usages of high society and the good manners which he sorely lacked. Whether he was enamored of Madeleine is not known. It is certain, however, that he was profoundly influenced by her and found her fascinating.

The relationship, however, was not destined to last long: Cyrano's father, tired of financing his son's follies, decided to pull tight the purse strings, whereupon Cyrano decided to enlist as a cadet with the Noble Guards of the Gascon Captain, Carbon de Casteljaloux, to whom he had been introduced by his ever faithful friend, Le Bret. Cyrano was wounded in battle at Mouzon in 1639; the following year he left the Cadets and became part of the regiment of the Counts, participating in the siege of Arras—a boring affair, as all sieges are. Cyrano and his companions spent their time smoking and playing cards, just as in the opening scene of the fourth act of Rostand's play. The wife of the newlywed young Count of Canvoye was very much in love with her husband, and a graphomaniac besides—she sent him as many as three letters a day. The Count, who was not very gifted as a writer, in order to hide his embarrassment, turned for help on more than one occasion to Cyrano, who supplied him with love poems to send to his beloved wife. It is probably this historic fact that furnished Rostand with the idea for the famous letter substitution by Cyrano for the handsome but almost illiterate Christian.

The boredom of the siege was broken by an enemy attack. Cyrano, in the front line, was stabbed in the throat by an enemy saber. When he regained consciousness in a rudimentary camp infirmary, he learned that among those who had fallen in battle was the Baron de Neuvillette, Madeleine's husband. The death of Christian at Arras is not, therefore, a literary invention, nor is the widow's withdrawal to a convent. When, in fact, Cyrano left the military service and returned home to convalesce in Paris, he learned that Madeleine was spending her life in prayer and penitence. He had the opportunity of seeing her in the Convent of the Holy Cross on the day that his sister, Catherine, took the veil. He scarcely recognized Madeleine: her mourning gown was of the poorest sort, her face was devastated by tears and fasting; and the former "peach complexion" was hidden under long gray hair that Madeleine no longer attempted to disguise by artificial coloring. In the face of this manifestation of profound humility, Cyrano experienced a sort of reverse exhibitionism; he fled from the convent, horrified, and vowed never to return.

The ex-Cadet of Gascony now lived as he could, in the intellectual circles of Paris, where he underwent the influence of the famous mathematician and materialist philosopher, Gassendi. Refusing all protectors, he preferred to gain his own reputation for libertine ideas and extravagance. He wrote two fantasies in prose, *Le Voyage dans la lune* and *L'Histoire des Etats de l'Empire du Soleil*, letters, maxims, and even a study of physics. Author also of a comedy *(Le Pédant joué)* and a tragedy *(La Mort d'Agrippine)* that he was unsuccessful in having presented, Cyrano finally was constrained to turn to a protector—Louis, Duke of Arpajon, Marquis of Séverac and Count of Rodez. Notwithstanding the Duke's protection, the presentation of his tragedy was a failure. The audience rioted on the first night because of an innocent line which Cyrano's enemies chose to interpret as a sacrilege. Presentations of the play were suspended and, as a result, requests for the text at the Charles de Sercy publishing house reached an all-time high. The Duke began to regret the protection he had accorded, and Cyrano, too, felt the weight of the attachment. A fortuitous accident—or a plot—hastened their separation: a beam fell from the roof of the ducal residence and struck the poet on the head; he was to remain for a year on the threshold of death. And this is the ambush that is freely evoked by Rostand in the fifth act of his play.

The good Le Bret undertook to have his injured friend transported to the home of a certain Tanneguy for treatment. Madeleine visited him there twice, but her words of comfort apparently must not have been much appreciated, since the dying Cyrano sent word to his cousin, Pierre de Cyrano, who lived in Lannois, begging him to come to fetch him and promising that he would not disturb him for too long—just a few days. Pierre answered the call of distress, arriving at Tanneguy's home on July 25th; Cyrano, wavering, rose from bed, got dressed, went downstairs, and was assisted into the waiting carriage. On July 28, 1655, just a few days later, he was, in fact, dead, in accordance with his promise to his cousin. Cyrano de Bergerac's was a first-class mind whose brilliant fantasies, ingenious scientific hypotheses, and bold religious and political views were prematurely interrupted. Rostand, by reviving him in his celebrated play, contributed much to his fame. Rostand's hero, however, is very different from the real Cyrano, even though many biographical elements in the play are exact and though there are significant similarities between the two figures.

Rostand merely develops the figure of the noble idealist who fights against the reality of ordinary life. His Cyrano, however, never admits to such a reality but creates his own world. In such a personal cosmos, the objective observer might judge him to be the loser, but Cyrano gains for himself his most precious ideal—*panache*. Cyrano's world comprises two existences: the life of each day and the life of love. He cherishes the highest concepts of life and duty; in them are contained the plot of the play and the story of his soul. Rostand dedicated the work to the *soul* of Cyrano. The play is an heroic comedy, which is very close to tragedy. As in a Molière play, not only is the sacrifice of a noble soul seen, but also the struggle of an heroic soul against all the evils of society and even against that love of idealism that can be harmful because of its own strength. From this point of view, Rostand's Cyrano surpasses the real one; love works miracles. It is this love that carries Roxane's soul to a higher level. Cyrano's idealism causes those who approach him to become idealistic, too. But the real tragedy lies in the fact that this idealistic love, which renders Roxane faithful to the memory of Christian, is the source of all of Cyrano's heroism and all his hatred for convention. In the end, it is also the cause of his death. What Cyrano loves so passionately is not Roxane—who, in truth, does not at all deserve his love, at least in the beginning of the play. He loves Love itself. He loves the fantasy that he has invented and which has become his ideal, personified by Roxane. The interest of the play, therefore, lies in the soul of Cyrano. To seize the essence of this great soul and to appreciate the true heroism of the comedy, an analysis of the internal and external figure of Rostand's creation is necessary.

Cyrano may be considered first as an able and clever man with a temperament that, once aroused, can manifest itself sweetly and paternally—but only in intimacy or in a deeply sincere relationship. Usually he is extremely violent. The most important external aspect of his character is the cult of the gesture, of which there are two kinds. First, there is the splendid gesture, the theatrical gesture, the execution of a duel while composing an improvised ballad, or marching at the head of a motley procession to fight single-handed against one hundred men. These are bravuras inspired by Cyrano's grotesque external appearance, but he executes them because he is full of life, energy and goodness—and is timid inside. He is a poet and a creator, but he senses his own ugliness and has lost his love for his own life. This explains the splendor of his verses. At this point, it is almost imperative to quote in their entirety Cyrano's memorable variations on the theme of his big nose:

> Aggressive: "Sir, if I had such a nose,
> I'd cut it off, so much 'twould cut me up."
> Friendly: "It oft must plunge, sir, in your cup;—
> Best make a goblet of a special shape."
> Descriptive: " 'Tis a rock,—a cliff,—a cape.
> A cape, quotha? Surely a promontory."
> Curious: "What is that thing,—let's have the story,—
> A tool box, or, perhaps, a writing case?"
> Gracious: "You must love birds to have a place
> Paternally prepared,—I call it sweet,—
> To make a safe perch for their tiny feet."
> Truculent: "Sir, be careful when you smoke,
> Lest you make trouble for all honest folk,—
> Lest neighbors run and cry, 'A chimney fire!' "
> Careful: "Pray hold your head a little higher,
> Else such a weight will surely make you fall."
> Solicitous: "Sir, take a parasol,
> Lest its bright hue be faded by the sun."
> Pedantic: "Aristophanes knew one,—
> Hippocampelephantecamelos

Was made to carry, certes, such a nose."
Lightly: "Why, friend, a most commodious rack
To hang one's hat,—where space will never lack."
Emphatic: "Fierce Euroclydon, behold,
Needs all his power to give that nose a cold."
Dramatic: " 'Tis the Red Sea when it bleeds."
Admiring: " 'Tis the sign the chemist needs."
Lyric: "A conche and you a triton, say?"
Simple: "A monument. When's visiting day?"
Respectful: "Come, the landed gentry greet.
Here's one who has a gable on the street."
Rustic: "Why look-a-here. A nose? I tell 'un
'Tis a prize turnip,—or a stunted melon."
Soldierly: "Charge, heavy artillery."
Practical: "Put it in the lottery.
Assuredly 'twould be, sir, the Grand Prize."
Or, last, like Pyramus, with streaming eyes:
"No wonder that nose blushes;—wicked traitor
Who mars his master, shaming his Creator."
Here are a few things, sir, you might have said,
Had you or wit or learning. But instead,
You wretched fop who trifle with your betters,
You have no spark of wit; and as for letters,
You have just four, to write you down a fool.
Had you one grain, from nature or from school,
Before these galleries you might have played
With some such fancies as myself displayed;—
—But not the fourth part of them all have spoke,
Nay, nor the half of one,—for I may joke,
Jest, as my mood or mockery may nerve me,—
But as I serve myself let no man serve me.[6]

The lines are a fine example of humor and verbal bravura, and yet they convey perfectly Cyrano's self-mockery and inner suffering.

In addition to the splendid gestures, there are Cyrano's heroic gestures, which render his soul so noble and great: the letters he writes for Roxane on behalf of Christian; the balcony scene, in which he directs the unfolding of the lovers' exchange all for his friend's benefit. These magnanimous gestures are so much more beautiful than the others because they are completely gratuitous. They are born of Cyrano's own personal pride and of his heroism. Perhaps the best example, however, of the heroic gesture is the

scene that so poignantly combines the comic and the tragic: the
scene in which Cyrano detains the Count de Guiche from entering
Roxane's home, where her marriage ceremony to Christian is being
performed—a ceremony that Cyrano wishes desperately would not
take place and yet which he desires fervently for his beloved Roxane's happiness. Pretending to fall heavily, as if from a great height,
and lying motionless as if stunned by his fall from the moon,
Cyrano intercepts the Count's approach and holds him enthralled
for the time necessary for Roxane and Christian to plight their troth.
Rostand has cleverly captured the flavor of the real Cyrano's *Le
Voyage dans la lune* and *L'Histoire des Etats de l'Empire du Soleil*
in the scene, which is worth quoting in part:

> I'm dizzy . . . giddy . . . for like a bomb
> I hurtled from the moon.
> . . . .
> Not metaphorically but with force.
> Centuries agone . . . or else, a minute, . . .
> How long I fell, I know not. I was in it . . .
> That saffron ball up yonder in the sky!
> . . . .
> Keep nothing from me. On what earthly site
> Have I descended like an aerolite?
> . . . .
> I came,—your pardon,—through a waterspout,
> Cloudburst, that left its spray. I have journeyed, sir.
> My eyes are full of stardust. Ha, . . . this spur
> Caught in a comet's tail. This golden tinge.
> Here, on my doublet, is a meteor's fringe.
> . . . .
> See, there, on my calf,—mark of a tooth?
> The Great Bear hit me. As I dodged, forsooth
> I missed the Trident but I fell ker-plunk!
> Into the Balances. See, they are sunk!
> They mark my weight. Look how the record lingers.
> If you should tweak my nose between your fingers,
> 'Twould prove a fount of milk . . .
> From the Milky Way.
> Would you believe, Sirius,—I saw this sight,—
> Puts on a cloudy nightcap every night?
> The Little Bear can't bite;—he tries to nip.

I broke a string in Lyra by a slip.
I mean to write my travels in a book.
These stars entangled in my mantle,—look,—
When I've recorded all my diverse risks,
These captured stars shall serve as asterisks.

. . . .

By six sure methods I can rise like vapor.
I could stand naked like a waxen taper,
Caparisoned with crystal phials clear,
Unstoppled, filled with summer's earliest tear,—
My body to the sunlight I'd expose,
And it were lifted as the dew arose.

GUICHE: Ho! That makes one way.

CYRANO: And again, I might
Draw winds into a vacuum,—keep it tight,—
Rarify them, by glowing mirrors, pressed
Isosahedron-wise within a chest.

GUICHE: Two!

CYRANO: Then, both mechanic and inventor, I
Make a steel grasshopper and let it fly
By swift explosions, till it fire me far
To the blue pastures of the farthest star.

GUICHE: Three!

CYRANO: Or, since smoke rises in its natural state,
I'd catch a globeful, equal to my weight.

GUICHE: Four!

CYRANO: Luna loves, what time her bow is narrow,
To suck beef-marrow, so I'd smear with marrow.

GUICHE: Five!

CYRANO: On an iron disc I'd stand with care,
And toss a lodestone lightly in the air.
That is a good way. When the iron flew,
Drawn by the magnet, as we nearer drew,
I'd catch the magnet,—toss it up! You see,
One might keep climbing through eternity.

GUICHE: Six! And all excellent. Now, tell me, pray,
Which method did you choose?

CYRANO: A seventh way!

GUICHE: Indeed! And what?

CYRANO: Give up! You'd never guess!

GUICHE: Stark mad, but most ingenious none the less.

CYRANO: . . . It is the ocean!
          When the moon moved the yearning tide to motion
          I lay out on the sands, wave-wet, and so
          My head was moved, and lifted . . . lifted slow,—
          Hair holds the water, sir,—and *very* slowly,
          I rose, just like an angel, stiff and holy.
          Effortless, splendid, high above all men
          I rose . . . I rose . . . I felt a shock. . . .
GUICHE: And then? . . .
CYRANO: . . . The time is up, Sir, and I set you free.
          The wedding's over.[7]

In the heroic gesture may be seen the tragedy of the man of
genius: Cyrano is a poet, a philosopher, an indomitable fencer and
an idealist; but he is not successful *because* he is heroic, *because* he
is idealistic, and *because* he fears ridicule. His philosophy, as he explains it to Le Bret, is: ". . . Let what will befall / Always I will be
admirable, in all."[8] The genuine Cyrano is the Cyrano of the *panache*. He desires to be "admirable in all"—and only for his own
satisfaction. This is the explanation of his profound sincerity. Even
though he may reiterate many times that it is beauty which he
loves, Cyrano loves sincerity and courage above all. He loves Christian mainly because he has made his promise to Roxane to protect
him, but also because Christian is courageous. He loves Le Bret
because he is sincere. He loves the cadets because they personify
courage. He loves the pastry cook, Ragueneau, because he is a poet
and writes sonnets on the paper bags in which he wraps his tarts and
pies. Cyrano's attitude toward women is the same: he shows esteem
for a woman of the lowest social rank and treats her as a princess
because she is kind and generous, but he has no sympathy for
Ragueneau's wife because she is harsh and insensitive to his poetry
and treats her husband badly.

With regard to Roxane, Cyrano has a completely different out-
look. At the beginning, his passion is a kind of poetic veneration for
her beauty; in her presence he remains wide-eyed and timid. When
he learns that it is not himself but rather Christian who is loved by
Roxane, his passion increases to the point of becoming poetry for
the sake of love. Passion renders Cyrano heroic because it infuses
into his noble heart the fire and warmth of his altruistic philosophy:

> . . . Self drops out of sight.
> For thy least good I would give all my own;—
> Aye, though thou knewst it not. . . . .[9]

Cyrano loves love more than he loves Roxane, but for him love is Roxane herself. His love is that of a man who has never known a woman intimately. He admits that he has never known "feminine sweetness."

At times, Cyrano is melancholy, but only toward the end of his life, as, for example, when Le Bret notices that he seems to be suffering. Cyrano starts, and cries out that he will never show others his suffering. All must appear heroic. During Roxane's last visit, looking at the falling leaves, he exclaims: "How well they fall!"[10], and later he speaks of "the fullness of Fate's mockery."[11] Cyrano is a man, a hero, from the beginning of the play to the end. He is Gascon only in appearance; within, he is a southerner, litigious, passionate, and a lover of theatrical poses. His is the temperament of Don Quixote.

As for Roxane, she is affected, very light, with little spiritual depth. She is romantic, but without the youthful simplicity of Sylvette in *Romantics*. Her beauty is legendary, like the far-off princess Melissinde's, and her lace handkerchief inspires the starving garrison at the siege of Arras just as the vision of the princess far away encouraged the feverish sailors to continue rowing. Roxane further resembles Melissinde in that neither would ever consider committing a great crime of love. Roxane seeks only an excessively refined sort of love. Little by little, however, the influence of Cyrano's idealism has an impact on her concept of life's values, giving rise to a deep spiritual evolution within her. Ultimately, she is able to say to Christian: "At last I love thee for thy soul alone!"[12] After Christian's death, she is faced with the cruel reality that there is nothing left in life for her, but she maintains an admirable calm. Subsequently, when she learns of Cyrano's love and exclaims: "I loved but once, and twice I lose my love!"[13], although the concept is affected, the cry comes from a heart genuinely in despair, and Roxane is tragically moving. In sum, the figure of the heroine represents a force in Cyrano's life; she is love personified. Just as Bertrand, in *The Princess Far Away*, is not easily defined or explain-

ed with respect to Melissinde, so the figure of Roxane is not easily
juxtaposed with respect to Cyrano.

Turning to the secondary characters as conceived by Rostand,
Christian de Neuvillette may be defined as a provincial youth, a bit
out of style, who does not dare to speak to Roxane because he knows
he lacks wit. He is very handsome and certainly is courageous
because he dares to do something that no other brave soldier would
even consider: tease Cyrano about his nose! But he is a simple
soldier. He becomes impatient in the role of the affected lover, yet
when Cyrano leaves him to his own devices, he is unable to do more
than stammer some banalities. In the end, he allows himself to be
killed in the siege in order to leave an open, free path for his friend.
Christian is genuinely sincere—and therefore is beloved by
Cyrano—but his role is reduced to being handsome and consequently being nothing but an obstacle in Cyrano's love life. In this
respect, he is the counterpart of Bertrand in *The Princess Far Away*.

Le Bret plays the role of the confidant. Embodying a spirit of
good sense, he is a kind of Sancho Panza at the side of Don Quixote.
Through the intimate conversations between Le Bret and Cyrano,
the latter's character is developed and his ideas and ideals are
revealed.

The last of the secondary characters is the Count de Guiche, a
true cavalier in Louis XII style, typifying the role of the mundane in
comedy. He lacks ideals, except for a sort of personal concept of
noblesse oblige, but his courage in battle inspires admiration. The
only effect that Cyrano's idealism produces in him is to render him
a bit dreamy at the end of the play, when he pronounces Cyrano's
eulogy. His dreaminess, however, is not an early manifestation of
the purification of a soul, but rather the expression of a weak and
egotistic character that feels some remorse:

> Envious . . . Yes!
> Sometimes, when one has made life's success,
> One feels,—not finding, God knows, much amiss,—
> A thousand small distastes, whose sum is this;
> Not quite remorse, but an obscure disorder. [14]

Groups and crowds of personages are part of the play, and indeed
Rostand shows extraordinary skill in harmonizing large numbers of
onlookers with the action of the main characters. The dramatic duel

scene and the exit procession are the most striking in *Cyrano de Bergerac;* the pastry cook surrounded by poets and cadets creates an additional unforgettable scene; and, finally, the group scene in the convent garden, under falling leaves, forms a scene of peace and tranquil joy mixed with a nuance of fatality.

Undoubtedly there are some defects in Rostand's masterpiece: too much refinement, too many theatrical gestures. Cyrano is perhaps too much the incarnation of the Romantic hero, with his contrasting physical ugliness and moral beauty. The poetry of the play is pure and lyric, however, because it is sincere. Rostand, the excessively refined stylist, is comfortable in his own preciosity. Rostand, the singer of heroic zeal, is comfortable in his Cyrano. The work, therefore, vibrates with preciosity, heroism, and poetic idealism. Moreover, as Patricia Williams maintains, the play is a strictly classical work in that it is faithful to the Aristotelian precepts, one of which is that a tragedy must be plausible. She affirms that Cyrano "is completely credible, and his actions are completely motivated by his convictions. He is true to life."[15]

The best excuse for Rostand's rhetoric and the best compliment to his dramatic sense are offered, however, by T. S. Eliot, who writes:

His rhetoric, at least, suited him at all times so well, and so much better than it suited a much greater poet, Baudelaire, who is at times as rhetorical as Rostand. . . . Is not Cyrano exactly in th[e] position of contemplating himself as a romantic, a dramatic figure? This dramatic sense on the part of the characters themselves is rare in modern drama. . . . Rostand had—whether he had anything else or not—this dramatic sense, and it is what gives life to Cyrano. It is a sense which is almost a sense of humour (for when any one is conscious of himself as acting, something like a sense of humour is present). It gives Rostand's characters—Cyrano at least—a gusto which is uncommon on the modern stage. . . . [I]n the particular case of Cyrano on Noses, the character, the situation, the occasion were perfectly suited and combined. The tirade generated by this combination is not only genuinely and highly dramatic: it is possibly poetry also.[16]

Rostand's *Cyrano of Bergerac* will continue to have meaning throughout the ages, will continue to move audiences everywhere, and probably will remain identified with the name of Edmond Rostand long after his other works have sunk into complete oblivion.

II   The Eaglet: *The Lyricism of a "Poor Child"*

Youth frequently inspired Rostand in his choice of heroes and heroines. In *The Eaglet*, it is not the joyful, amorous youth of *Romantics* that is seen, but rather the immaturity and fragility of a young boy, Franz. Known both as the Duke of Reichstadt and the King of Rome, Franz was the son of Napoleon I and Maria Luisa (the daughter of the Archduke Francis I of Austria and Napoleon's second wife). He lived from 1811 to 1832. His claim to the paternal throne of France as Napoleon II (after Napoleon's first abdication in 1814) was at first nominal; a year later, instead, the title was formally established. In his declaration of June 22, 1815, dictated to his brother, Luciano, Napoleon spoke the following words: "My life is finished and I proclaim my son, under the name of Napoleon II, Emperor of the French." The words were repeated aloud by the Emperor himself before the nation's House of Representatives, which recognized the sovereignty of Napoleon II. Even before Waterloo, the divisive maneuver had been suggested by Joseph Fouché, Minister of Police under the Empire (who betrayed Napoleon after the Hundred Days and kept his ministry under the Restoration). Fouché's intention was probably to split the loyalties of the allies between father and son. By bestowing his crown on his son, Franz (who had been living for a year in Austria with his grandfather), Napoleon made some concession to the scruples of Francis I, one of the signers of the declaration of Vienna against the "usurper Bonaparte." The gesture helped to extract his son somewhat from the close custody of Metternich; Austria did not, however, release its grasp on the "Eaglet," fearing in him the bellicose blood of his father. At first it was decided that he would become "Prince of Parma," with hereditary rights (entrusted to his mother, Maria Luisa) to the Duchy of Parma, Piacenza and Guastalla. Then, instead, the title of the Duke of Reichstadt was bestowed on him, with compensation for the loss of effective sovereignty over any territory in the form of lands and rents.

After Waterloo, Fouché passed definitively to the side of the Bourbons, and it was principally due to his pressure that the June 22, 1815 proclamation became, for all practical purposes, a dead letter.

Adolph Hitler, during the course of his exercise of power, made one sentimental gesture toward the French: immediately after his lightning victory over France in July 1940, he ordered that the remains of the King of Rome be removed from the Capucin crypt (Kapuzinerkirche) in Vienna, where they had been reposing for over a century among the tombs of the Hapsburgs. Where the Eaglet's body was once entombed now lies his mother, who died in 1867. Hitler gave the order for Franz' remains to be solemnly transported to Paris—to the Invalides—for interment with those of the Emperor Napoleon exactly one hundred years after the return to Paris of Bonaparte's ashes. He intended this spectacular form of "restitution" to be not so much an act of posthumous justice as a move to attract the sympathy of the French, who have always been sensitive to the memory of Napoleon. The voyage of the remains of the Eaglet took place, however, among general indifference and aloofness, in a Europe racked by war.

A few months later, however, references to the King of Rome began to increase because a nobleman of Trento, Baron de Moll, in going through his family archives, discovered an important document: the diary of one of his ancestors, Captain Giancarlo de Moll, who had lived in the military "household" of the Duke of Reichstadt and had kept watch over him during the long illness that ended in his premature death. The diary was published; it is a cut and dried document with no embellishment yet extraordinarily interesting. It constitutes the most significant testimony that has been preserved in connection with the death of the King of Rome. Precisely because of the lack of sympathy on the part of de Moll, who did not expect his words to be published, and because of the cold detachment of his tone and the indifference with which he speaks of the progress of the illness that was slowly taking Franz to his death, the reconstruction of a fairly accurate portrait of the Duke of Reichstadt is possible. Napoleon II is stripped of his Romantic veils, but he is infinitely more human and more pathetic than the "Prisoner Eaglet" of the Bonaparte tradition. Even now, more than a quarter of a century after the publication of the de Moll diary, the legends of the "Austrian feathers" of Carducci's ode, and of the tempestuous loves that seem to have led Napoleon's son to an early death, are difficult to surrender to reality. The pale, sickly youth, dead at the age of twenty, without having brought salvation to France, remains a tenacious image. Today, his mortuary mask is exposed in the room of Schoenbrunn Palace which had twice been occupied by Napoleon I. Overlooking the vast and impressive gardens of the palace, the room contains, besides the mask, only a stuffed bird—symbol of the Eaglet and, as the Viennese guide today will announce nostalgically, Franz' only friend.

The correspondence between Franz and his mother, Maria Luisa of Austria, was continuous and affectionate. They wrote to each other indiscriminately in the two languages in which they were both fluent—French and German. (Franz also spoke Italian rather well—a language that was coming more and more into favor at the Court of Vienna despite the origins of the "usurper Bonaparte.") Some of the boy's letters to his mother are extremely bellicose and justify the phrase pronounced by the old Prince of Ligne who, meeting him as a child of four, found him already to have "military eyes." In fact, the nineteen-year-old Duke wrote to his mother on March 25, 1830:

[P]erhaps I shall be able to participate [in the maneuvers] next year at the head of my battalion. What a great day that will be! All my desires end there, because to push them as far as the joy of a war would be excessive audacity, especially during these times. . . . In truth, I have the sad foreboding that I shall die without having received the baptism of fire. I have already made my decision in case of this terrible eventuality. I shall put into my will that my bier should be brought into the first battle that should occur, so that my soul will have the consolation, wherever it may be, of hearing whistling around its bones the bullets it has so often desired. . . .[17]

The passage is puerile, and typical of a child who enjoys war-play in the shadow of Napoleon. But in these few lines there is an obscurely prophetic tone. Like a shiver, the presentiment of a precocious death runs through them.

One of Franz's more noteworthy qualities was his independence of judgment. He did not repudiate any aspect of his father's moral heritage despite his Austrian indoctrination. One of his dearest friends, Anton Prokesch-Orten, found him one day absorbed in the reading of the *Memorial of Saint Helena,* which contains Napoleon's testament. The Eaglet read out loud to Anton the fourth paragraph, in which Napoleon exhorts his far-off son never to forget that he was born a French prince. "That," he added," is the rule of conduct of my entire life."

At first glance, Franz, Duke of Reichstadt, looked like a true Hapsburg, with the characteristic protruding upper lip, blond hair and blue eyes. Contrary to most observers, however, Marshal Auguste Viesse de Marmont, the Duke of Ragusa whom the Bonapartists referred to as the "traitor of Essonnes" because he negotiated secretly with the Allies to force Napoleon's abdication, discerned a physical resemblance between Franz and his father. The Eaglet's facial structure, his gestures, and a certain way of inclining his head to one side, were clearly inherited from Bonaparte. None of Napoleon's Corsican ruggedness, however, had passed to his son. That young figure, so full of charm and attractiveness, was, unfortunately, of an alarming fragility. Although there were already some worries about his health in 1826, when the boy was fifteen years old, fears abated after his summer vacation in Austria.

They reappeared, however, five years later, and much more intensely. It was then that gossip began about the young Duke's "excesses" which would inevitably undermine his health. In the liberal circles of Europe, specific accusations were leveled against Metternich and the Austrian court for actually encouraging these excesses in the cynical hope of getting rid of "the Son of the Man." Names were mentioned; the most persistent were those of the dancer Fanny Elssler and the Countess Nadine Károlyi, née Kaunitz. These ladies were, however, merely the objects of a schoolboy's infatuations. Only one woman seems to have inspired a deep sentiment in Franz: Princess Sofia of Bavaria, wife of the Archduke Francis Charles, a maternal uncle of the Duke. Sofia was that "aunt with cousin's eyes," of whom Rostand speaks in such fine imagery. Some historians do not hesitate to attribute to Franz the paternity of Sofia's two sons, Francis Joseph and Maximilian, born a few days before the Eaglet's death. The Court of Vienna had recourse to Sofia so that etiquette should be preserved until the end, and this historic fact is freely evoked by Rostand in his play. The sick Duke not only had to receive the last sacraments of the Church, but he had to receive them in public, in the presence of the Court and the blood Princes. Sofia, eight months pregnant, found a plausible motive for the ceremony, without alarming the dying Franz. Proposing to confess and take holy communion in order to invoke the benediction of God on her childbirth, she urged Franz to do likewise.

Only a few intimates were present in the room, but outside a small crowd hedged around in silence. At a certain moment, during the receiving of the sacraments, the doors opened soundlessly and then closed again. Etiquette was saved. The end came shortly after. Franz's last words, in German, were addressed to his mother: "Ich gehe unter, Mutter, Mutter!" ("Mother, Mother, I am going under!").[18]

Such, then, is the real story of Franz, Duke of Reichstadt and King of Rome. Possibly Rostand used it as the basis for his second masterpiece because in Franz's biography he found inspiration for the negative counterpart of the swashbuckling hero. After the success of *Cyrano of Bergerac*, Rostand felt he had to create something even better, which would have to take the form of a reverse image, since no figure could possibly outdo Cyrano. An ascending creative parabola will be observed in his successive works, reaching its symbolic and lyric apex with *Chanticleer*.

While he was still working on *Cyrano of Bergerac*, *Le Roi de Rome* by a certain von der Pforten was being performed at the Royal Theater in Berlin. Moreover, the figure of the Eaglet—France's Hamlet—had occupied a place in Rostand's heart for a long time. As a boy, he slept in a bed over which hung a portrait of the Duke of Reichstadt:

This portrait, he said, had become a sort of friend to me. I saw it from my bed, in the morning, on opening my eyes. It was he who presided over my studies, when I was working alone at my little table. He was present at my first readings, my first dreams, and at my first emotions.[19]

Rostand felt a premonition of his own future in the destiny of the young Duke. The child was enchained by the past triumph of his father and lived in unceasing anguish. Rostand, after *Cyrano of Bergerac*, would never succeed in freeing himself from the anguish of creativity except by creating a new masterpiece.

There were other reasons for the choice of the story of the Duke of Reichstadt. In the dedicatory note of his collection of poems, *Les Musardises*, Rostand declared his love for all those who are mocked, scorned, and disinherited, and for all those who, desiring to do well, in the end achieve nothing. In Rostand's eyes, the Duke of Reichstadt was one who had been mocked and scorned; Fate had decreed that he should accomplish nothing. Ten years after *Cyrano of Bergerac*, then, *The Eaglet* appeared, dedicated to the "two Maurices" in these words:

> Great God! Here is no cause
> Defended or reviled.
> I only bid you pause
> To pity a poor child.[20]

An historic drama in six acts, the play may be considered a masterpiece of lyricism rather than a masterpiece of drama. It is difficult to say whether it is a psychological drama or a kind of dramatized epic poem. Love is relegated to a secondary level, yet the work breathes a certain sentimentality because Rostand simply wanted to bring "the story of a poor child" to the stage. While the plot of *Cyrano of Bergerac* is based on two big lies, heroic and full of verve, *The Eaglet* is not very heroic. It is the tragedy of an unfulfilled dream, and nothing else. Cyrano lived his life scornful of the circumstances surrounding him. He created his personal reality and came very close to triumph even when he failed. The Eaglet hardly lived. He merely created his dream. His desire was to cultivate a legend (like Melissinde in *The Princess Far Away*), but the circumstances of life did not allow his dream to be realized. The illusion did not serve the cause of action. The Eaglet stalls. His hesitation is fatal. In the first of the two sonnets entitled "In the Crypt of the Capucins, at Vienna," found at the end of the play, Rostand declares:

> In vain the scribbler searches what to write.
>   The Poet knows. Historians repeat.
>   My verse may perish, but Time cannot cheat
> Wagram of that pale form against the light.
>
> . . . Tis not Legend always that deceives.
> A dream is truer far than yellowed leaves.
> Sleep. You were Youth. You were Napoleon's son.[21]

As for the dramatic construction of *The Eaglet*, like *The Woman of Samaria*, its acts are really tableaus, and each is evocative of the eagle symbol. The entire work may be considered as a sequence of events rather than the evolution of a character. The principal set-

ting is nineteenth-century Austria in the Palace of Schoenbrunn, at
the Court of the Archduke, Francis I. The first act, or prologue, entitled "Fledgling Wings," is set in Maria Luisa's villa in Baden,
near Vienna, where everything French is interdicted. A conversation between Metternich and Frederick of Gentz reveals Fouché's
intentions of proclaiming the Duke of Reichstadt Napoleon the Second. Metternich is unperturbed by the report, confident that Maria
Luisa will prevent the infiltration of the news and the hatching of
any plots that might upset her ingenuous tranquillity. At most she
has smuggled in a French tailor and a modiste for herself and her
son. Against a backdrop of music, entertainment, and festivities are
heard conversations with political undertones. A loud cry of "Long
live Napoleon!" brings panic to the villa, which is quickly con-
trolled by Metternich. The friends of the Duke of Reichstadt beg
him to return to France as Emperor of the French, but he does not
feel up to the task and asks for "three hundred sleepless nights" in
order to prepare himself. The Duke's tutors arrive on the scene for
the daily Austrian history lesson, which Franz boldly and deftly
turns into an apotheosis of his father to the consternation and
mystification of his teachers, who have censored all of their pupil's
reading matter. Maria Luisa appears on the scene; Franz, in a fit of
rebellion, rejects his mother's heritage and claims the blood of only
a Corsican lieutenant in his veins. But he immediately becomes
tender once again and hurries his superbly clad mother off to the
dance, begging her to forget and forgive his frenzy and delirium.
Frederick of Gentz leads a closely veiled woman into the Duke's
chamber: it is the dancer, Fanny Elssler, who, in Franz's arms,
recites memorized details of the Imperial Guard's heroic acts, for
she is the source of the imprisoned Eaglet's knowledge of
Napoleonic history.

   In the second act—"Fluttering Wings"—a year has elapsed. The
Duke has established his work room in the palace chamber used by
Napoleon the First when—twice—he occupied Schoenbrunn.
Franz's close friend, the Chevalier of Prokesch-Osten, has been
brought to the palace, thanks to the influence of the Archduchess,
Franz's aunt. The Duke laments that his partisans have forgotten
him, but Prokesch encourages him to make preparations for his
return to France. Marshal Marmont, Napoleon's faithful soldier,
Seraphin Flambeau, and the Countess Camerata, Franz's cousin,

are all plotting together for Napoleon II's triumphal re-entry into Paris.

The third act is entitled "Spreading Wings;" in it, hopes are raised that the Duke of Reichstadt will find the strength to flee Austria. The Emperor Franz is giving audiences to the citizens attired in their Bohemian, Tyrolean, and other national costumes, waiting to present their petitions before the throne. A shepherd enveloped in a great mantle presents his paper to the Emperor:

> A shepherd of Tyrol,
> Orphaned, despoiled and driven from his home
> By ancient enemies, desires to come
> Back to its woods, its skies . . .
> And to his father's land.

The Chamberlain asks the name of the shepherd, who stands erect and shouts: "The Duke of Reichstadt, and his land is France!"[22] His grandfather rebukes him, but then the two begin to reminisce about times past and their deep love for each other. Franz begs his grandfather to give in to his whims once more and allow him to go to Paris, so that he will be able to claim: "This is my grandson, Emperor of France!" The Emperor agrees, and they joyfully embrace, but Metternich appears to thwart their dream. Grandfather and grandson separate like children caught in mischief. The Emperor informs Metternich that he wishes Franz to reign; Metternich accepts on the condition that liberty be muzzled in France and that Napoleon II reign as an Austrian puppet. The Emperor Franz and Metternich fall into agreement, whereupon the Duke of Reichstadt recoils from them in horror. That evening, he sets the signal for the plotters: one of his father's little black hats, placed on the half-open map of Europe. Flambeau stands guard at the Duke's door. Metternich enters, does not see Flambeau in the shadows, and begins to address the hat in a tirade that gives way to an outburst of pure malevolence against Napoleon. Flambeau steps into the moonlight and stands motionless in the classic pose of a grenadier. Metternich recoils and rubs his eyes, thinking he is having an hallucination. Flambeau pretends that the year is 1809 and the French are quartered in Schoenbrunn; Metternich puts his finger into the flame of one of the candles to test whether he is dreaming.

Flambeau plays his part superbly, but when the Duke's chamber door opens and Flambeau proclaims in a sonorous voice: "Emperor Napoleon!" there is seen on the threshold the trembling form of a poor child in a white nightgown, slender and coughing—and Metternich recovers his composure. The Austrian Chancellor flings insults at Franz—"you have the little hat, but not the head"—and succeeds in convincing him of his inherent weakness. Cruelly evoking his ill-fated forebears, Metternich breaks Franz's pride and determination, and at the end of the act, the Duke falls to the ground, a lamentable white heap whose little strength has failed him.

In the fourth act—"Bruised Wings"—the curtain rises on a masquerade ball in the Park of Schoenbrunn. From behind their dominoes, Metternich and Sedlinsky, the prefect of police, discuss the plot which they expect the conspirators to execute during the evening. Metternich has no fear, because he is certain that Franz will remain in hiding and avoid the ball because his pride has been hurt. The Duke does, however, appear at the ball with his friend, Prokesch, but clearly trailing bruised wings. He agonizes over the fact that all his race has had its vein of madness and that he is foredoomed to shadows and despair. Accidentally observing an intimacy between his mother and the Count of Bombelles, Franz is suddenly filled with an upsurge of filial love for Napoleon. He seizes the Count by the throat and flings him to the ground. The gesture saves him from despondency and allows him to face Metternich once again with pride and insolence. Plans are laid for his escape to the Field of Wagram and his subsequent triumphal entry into Paris.

The fifth act—"Broken Wings"—opens with Franz's exultant words: his soul has become vast, he anxiously awaits the sight of his throne, and he already relishes his power. The conspirators gather around him; the Eaglet's foot is in the stirrup ready for the flight. At this moment, however, he is warned that the life of his cousin, the Countess Camerata, who has been posing as the Duke because of their close resemblance, is imperilled. The Duke insists on going to her aid—and his hesitation loses the conspirators' cause. Flambeau stabs himself and lies dying on the Field of Wagram "among the slain, / First for the father,—this time for the Son."[23] The Duke urgently and vividly re-creates Napoleon's battle in order to bring back a cherished and glorious past. Flambeau's last moments are peaceful, for his death comes in the midst of an illusion of victory. The Duke, himself transported by the fantasy he created for Flambeau, is finally brought back to reality by the approach of his Austrian regiment. Like an automaton, he leads the soldiers, giving his orders in the voice of an Austrian officer.

The sixth act (epilogue), entitled "Folded Wings," is set at Schoenbrunn in the Duke's bedchamber. In the feverish disorder of the sick room stands out a small bronze statue of Napoleon the First. The Archduchess, with forced gaiety, visits the horribly wasted Duke who, the Doctor informs her, "takes his milk well." The compliment offends the dying Franz, who "had burned for endless fame, / To shine with warriors, heroes of that ilk," and is "praised for the way in which one takes one's milk!"[24] The Archduchess succeeds in persuading Franz to observe court custom by attending Mass together and taking the sacrament. The Imperial Family looks on unobserved during the elevation of the host, and in the moment of profound emotion and perfect silence, even Metternich is touched by the nobility of the dying Eaglet. In a low, deep whisper, Metternich says: ". . . Oh he was a gallant prince! / . . . Not only to the Lamb of God I kneel."[25] When Franz becomes aware of the room full of people observing him, with calm and supreme majesty he bids his "Austrian family" to leave him, quoting to them the words from the *Memorial of Saint Helena:*

> "My son is born a French prince. Let him be
> A French prince unto death." Be it known
> That I obey. Farewell.[26]

The great vermilion cradle of the King of Rome is brought into the chamber and placed beside the bed of the Duke, who puts his hand between the cradle and the bed, uttering the deeply moving lines:

> My life lies in that space.
> . . . And Fate has shed
> In that dark, narrow space that holds my story,
> No single ray of all that blaze of glory![27]

Franz requests that French folk songs be sung to him and that the story of the proclamation of the King of Rome be read to him as he dies. The Duke's head falls forward; his last two words are: "Mama!" and "Napoleon."

In a drama of this type, interest centers on the possible actions to be carried out and on the sequence of events—not on the character of the Duke nor on that of Metternich, which are pre-established from the outset. The figure of Seraphin Flambeau is a memorable one, but his principal *raison d'être* is just to keep the play moving. He is a zealous, active soldier, whose energy is lacking in the Duke's own temperament. Franz finds inspiration in Flambeau and thereby nourishes his own hallucinations. *The Eaglet* is the narrative of a young man locked in struggle with his dreams of grandeur and with his sick body and vacillating temperament, in a hostile, foreign environment which is tragically indifferent to his struggle. Austrian indifference during his lifetime was matched by French indifference to the return of his remains in 1940. The Duke of Reichstadt never made his mark in the world; shadows and obscurity were his destiny, as he himself was able to predict.

Franz, Duke of Reichstadt, is a new Hamlet, but without the philosophy—the philosophy of gloom—of his predecessor. He is possessed of a double heritage: in his veins runs the blood of Bonaparte and the blood of old Austria. He is a Bonaparte with blond hair: "I've something blonde within that frightens me."[28] He has the nervous, sickly temperament of his mother. He is "too princely;" he never smiles; he is "blonde like Saint George;" "he seems not to be alive." On his own confessions, he is nothing but "a remembrance within a phantom." He is a Romantic hero, like Chatterton, and the weak side of his nature is revealed in a hundred ways. He is as excitable as a child when, for example, he finds the set of painted wooden soldiers; his Tyrol shepherd disguise, donned in order to request help from his grandfather, is nothing but a childish game. He seems to be playing a puerile role even on his deathbed, when he allows his imagination to depict his own funeral ceremony. This weak, Romantic hero, however, erupts with energy in a sort of burst of wrath (for example, when he declares himself to be a "living Wagram"), but these flings are of short duration and produce no concrete results. The most dramatic of them is the one in which he throws himself in fury against the Count of Bombelles, who has lightly kissed the shoulder of his mother. Franz recoils, astonished by his own act, and passes his hand over his brow, saying: "It was not I who laid that braggart low. / The Corsican leapt out and dealt the blow!"[29] Ultimately, Franz realizes that his zeal takes shape only in his dreams; it fades whenever he attempts to put it into action. His dreams are grandiose and heroic, but his own soul inspires loss of faith in himself, and he lives with an inferiority complex. The Duke of Reichstadt created by Rostand has no heroic qualities and he knows that posterity will create a distorted image of him:

> When History tells the story of my life,
> No one will see my dreams, fierce, stormy, wild, . . .
> They will see a go-cart, and a solemn child,
> A child not even crying for the moon,
> Holding the globe—but as a toy balloon![30]

In *The Woman of Samaria*, Jesus was passionate and at the same time his life, his goodness, his perfection, and all his divinity permitted him to produce miracles. In *The Princess Far Away*, Joffroy Rudel and Bertrand were courageous, and they were also poets. Cyrano was a swordsman, a poet, and stronger than those who envied him. The Duke, however, is nothing but the son of Napoleon. He is a dying soul possessed of a grandiose dream, a figure whose action is entirely inner, whereas the actions of those who have created their own life make themselves felt beyond their inner life. The action of the drama does not develop as an outgrowth of the Duke's behavior; he acts only when everything has been prepared for him by others. Once, in the middle of the drama, he thinks he has the power to act, but in desperation renounces his grandiose dreams to become nothing but a Don Juan. He discovers that he can have power over women only. The psychological study of the Eaglet is excellent, but the manner of presentation spoils the effect and produces an atmosphere of melodrama. Eloquent flings are followed by hesitation and inactivity; a lively hope is followed by a premature death. The Eaglet could not take flight toward France, the country of his Ideal. He dies, and nothing remains of his effort. Doubtless, the figure of the Duke was symbolic of the wave of feeling that swept Europe around 1830. It was an era of sentiment rather than of reason, of dream rather than of action, of timid veneration rather than of heroic admiration, of tragedy rather than of triumph. For this reason, it is difficult to distinguish clearly between the historic Duke and the legendary one. The deeply Romantic poets of the period saw in him the worthy son of Napoleon, whose energy and strong will clashed against the walls of his prison. They made of him a legendary martyr, a symbol of their own feeling of limitation in the face of hard reality. In this climate, the historian's objectivity was lost.

The two characters who arouse the most interest through their often melodramatic actions are Prince Metternich and Seraphin Flambeau. Metternich maintains close surveillance over the Duke, who is *"not-a-prisoner-but"* just let him try "[t]o speak behind closed doors with no one near, / That mushroom there would sprout a listening ear."[31] At night, Metternich penetrates into every corner of the castle, letting himself into every room with his pass-key; he is the spy who spies on the spies. From time to time, he demonstrates the quasi-diabolic skill of the old diplomat. To emphasize his non-heroic aspect, Rostand has created two scenes in the third act that deserve mention: one is the scene in which Metternich pronounces his long tirade over Napoleon's little hat. As he speaks, his hatred for Napoleon's greatness and virtue mount to the point where he loses his usual self-possession and takes the apparition of the grenadier (Flambeau in soldier's costume) for reality, believing he has gone back twenty years in time. The other scene is the one in which he attempts to break the pride of "this terrible child." All his capacity for cruelty and evil is revealed. Metternich is cold, diabolically clever, deprived of any dream or illusion. He is the personification of harsh, earthly logic, and he thereby constitutes the main obstacle in the path of the chimerical Duke.

Seraphin Flambeau, defender of the oppressed, as excessively and outrageously faithful to the son of Napoleon as he had been to the father, is perhaps the most captivating of the secondary characters in the play. It is he who exhorts the Duke to return to France, where youth will rally to him singing Béranger's songs. Admirably courageous, a conspirator in love with liberty and with his country, Flambeau has suffered privation and anguish in his desire for glory and for service to the "little corporal." Full of heroism, condemned to death a thousand times in contempt of court, he has the great defect of "always doing a little more than is necessary." He echoes Cyrano of Bergerac, fighting with a rose in his ear. Certainly,

Flambeau is more brusque and less poetic than Cyrano, and he is not a hero who lives in and shapes the present in the mold he desires. Flambeau lives in the glorious past of great victories and tragic sufferings. The spirit of Cyrano is most visible in the scene at the door of the Duke's chamber: donned in his old grenadier's uniform, he forgets that it is not Napoleon the great who is sleeping on the other side of the closed door, until he is taken by surprise by Metternich. Flambeau's lyricism is real, however, while that of Cyrano is slightly willfully excessive. Cyrano, in other words, consciously seeks the *recherché*, whereas Flambeau does not.

The strong contrast between the spirit of Flambeau and that of the Duke appears clearly in the sublime and unforgettable scene on the battlefield of Wagram. After the failure of the conspiracy, Flambeau lies dying, a victim of his own hand, while the Duke urgently tries to recall the past by relating the progress of Napoleon's battle:

> THE DUKE: We are at Wagram. Just before you fell
> Davoust's division crumpled Neusiedel.
> The Emperor with field glasses watches all
> You got a bayonet thrust. I saw you fall
> And bore you to this slope. . . .
> FLAMBEAU: (*struggling*): I am choking! Water! . . .
> Can . . .you . . . see
> The . . . Emperor?
> THE DUKE: He moves his hand.
> FLAMBEAU: (*closing his eyes, peacefully*): A victory![32]

The Duke's auto-suggestion is a really poetic creation. He produces an illusion in which Flambeau can die with confidence. This is the grand finale to the inglorious catastrophe of the Eaglet and to the illusory life of Franz who, later, on his own deathbed, creates a moving and admirable scene, playing games on the threshold of death in a style worthy of Cyrano's *panache*.

As with all of Rostand's plays, the reader is left with a feeling of insufficient psychological development of the characters. The author's genius reveals itself rather in the memorable pictures that capture a state of being or a particular gesture. Rostand is, above all, a love poet; in *The Eaglet,* he was constrained to put love on a secondary level. Even though love is always very close to an inner, sentimental dream, Rostand nevertheless uses it to accentuate the weakness and uselessness in the character of the Duke. The Eaglet is loved by the devoted Thérèse of Lorget; by his mother, Maria Luisa (who does not understand her son's anguish and who instead amuses herself by listening to light chit-chat at the palace balls); by the carefree dancer, Fanny Elssler; he is loved, indeed, by all women, except the Countess Camerata, an exceptional figure who assumes the proportions of a Cornelian heroine. About her, the Tailor says:

> She who delights to seem untamed and wild,
> Unarmoured Amazon whose proud young face
> Is living seal of her exalted race;
> Fences; breaks thoroughbreds; dares anything.[33]

The Countess Camerata attempts to incite the Eaglet to action. The moment he vacillates, she cries out:

> . . . Be gone! Ah me,
> Sir, if your Father were but here to see
> This sickly lad who wavers, doubts and frets
> How you would make him shrug his epaulettes![34]

In conclusion, I would say that Rostand's *The Eaglet* is a defective masterpiece. There are too many elements of preciosity in it, too many details and excessive refinements that are not essential: the dominoes at the ball, Legions of Honor, overabundant verses on Napoleon's tricolor and star, etc. There are too many disguises: Flambeau is disguised as an Austrian spy or as Neptune; the Eaglet as a Tyrolean shepherd in order to hand his petition to the Austrian Emperor; the Countess as the Duke, etc. There are too many Romantic antitheses in the pale, sickly child who makes his appearance on the scene at the height of the dramatic moment when Metternich expects Napoleon to emerge from the bedchamber. There are too many superfluous literary allusions, weighed down with alliterations, as, for example:

> Each breeze brings in a branch; with every breath
>   —Oh miracle to madden a Macbeth!—
> Not only does the forest march to me,

It swiftly dances in its ecstasy!
Borne on this sweet wind, lo, the forest flies![35]

On the other hand, and despite certain passages in which the
dialogue is too concise, *The Eaglet* contains the great qualities of
Rostand's art: lyricism and sincerity. It is a new lyricism, neither
affected nor Romantic, but rather sentimental—as it should be in a
Court whose atmosphere of music, color, languor and love, so well
rendered by Rostand, serves to obfuscate any heroic idealism and
zeal. Nevertheless, even if it is sometimes over-sentimental, the
feeling of sincerity that prevades such lyricism is inescapable.

The Eaglet has great dreams, noble sentiments, lofty aspirations,
and dares to defy the Austrian eagle with grandiose concepts:

O eagle black,
Two-headed bird with cruel, weary sight,
O Austrian eagle, world-worn bird of night,
An Eagle of the day swept through your path,
And,—fluttering wildly in your fear and wrath,—
Not daring to believe, bird black and old,
You see one eaglet sprouting wings of gold![36]

In the end, however, when everything slides away before his eyes
that are closing in death, he returns to the earthy solidity of the old
French popular songs. There is no progression of interest in the
play, as has already been stated, but Rostand's intention must not
be lost sight of: he wished to paint the portrait of a poor child who
wanted to outdo himself, a wistful child who would have liked to
make history but lived with his face pressed against the glass of the
palace of Schoenbrunn. The inner energy of Napoleon's son flowed
forth in a personal lyricism. His aspirations were grandiose and sentimental but completely sincere and colored by that fervor of youth
that made the heart of every Frenchman palpitate. All of France
became mother to that poor child, the Duke of Reichstadt.

CHAPTER 5

The Late Dramatic Works

IN the course of these analyses of Rostand's plays, the thread of a philosophy is discernible, spun around moods and gestures rather than a regular, systematic exposition of ideas. The works have transmitted definite, perceptible shades of meaning, and even though they are not always lyrical, emotion and a spirit of *panache* are consistently felt. Youthful idealism was seen on an April evening in *Romantics;* the dream of a medieval knight errant in *The Princess Far Away;* religious inspiration in an historic, Biblical parable, *The Woman of Samaria;* the deep, living impression of a dream in action executed by a noble, fervent character—Cyrano of Bergerac; and, finally, the sentimental, historic lyricism of a poor child, the Eaglet.

There remain to be examined Rostand's last great masterpiece, which is an apotheosis of his dramatic work and best expresses lyricism of action and thought—*Chanticleer;* and his posthumous *The Last Night of Don Juan,* which was written in 1910 for the actor, Le Bargy, who was performing for the last time at the Théâtre Français. Published in 1921, three years after Rostand's death, the play was produced a year later and proved to be a complete failure.

I Chanticleer: *"Who loses the Great Dream must die"*

Chanticleer is a symbolic poem in which I have used animals to evoke and relate the sentiments, passions and dreams of men. My Cock is not, properly speaking, a comic hero. He is the character that I have created to express my own dreams and to allow a bit of myself to re-live before my eyes. . . . Chanticleer is, if you will, something like the story of the human effort: the creative effort locked in struggle with the evil of creating, and all that this evil contains in the form of disappointments, hopes, sorrows, gratifications, great or small.[1]

The world of *Chanticleer* is a human world, then, where men live under the guise of animals. The play is a thesis work and the plot is of the simplest, yet Rostand worked on it for ten years, only to have it coldly received by the Parisian public. Perhaps the spectators were disconcerted by the fact that "the people of the play are small;" perhaps they were taken off their guard by the very modern technique of the Director of the Play rushing on stage to stop the raising of the curtain and calling to his chief carpenter to lower the magic wall "of glass that shows the size we men prefer." The curtain finally does rise, however, at the Woodpecker's three strokes, and "Aesop . . . fill[s] the prompter's box."[2]

Regardless of how audiences may react to the staged play, it is the reading of the text and the study of the figure of the Cock that are of interest here. Chanticleer plays the role of the hero in the fantastic melodrama; the heroine is the Pheasant Hen; and the villain in this symbolic world is represented by the figure of the Fighting Cock, White Pile.

The setting is a barnyard, where dwell all the poultry—hens, pullets, cockerels, chicks, ducks, and turkeys—all of whom love and admire Chanticleer; the good dog, Patou; and the old hen that hatched Chanticleer—"my, your, his, her, our, and their Cock," according to the envious Blackbird, who speaks Parisian slang:

> I sling my slang almighty well, I think,
> A Paris sparrow taught me. Slinging ink
> And slinging slang are all the rage in Paris . . . .[3]

Blackbird tries to be witty and sophisticated but turns out to be simply cynical and ridiculous. Faithful Patou would like "to dye his black coat red!" Blackbird speaks jeeringly of Chanticleer and taunts him by maintaining that there is nothing easier to create than a Cock. The recipe is of the simplest:

> You take a Honfleur melon for the torso;
> For legs, asparagus of Argenteuil:
> Bayonne pimento head, as I'm a merle!
> Currants of Bar-le-Duc for eyes; for tail,
> Rouen leeks, curved, blue-green. Lest Soissons fail,
> He has two tiny beans for ears. And so
> Behold your Cock complete![4]

Nevertheless, he admits, "I criticize details, . . . admire him in block."[5] Chanticleer is haughty but tender, proudly dignified, and courageous. He loves Light and Beauty so much that he declares to the Sun:

> I worship thee! Thou fillest the air with posies;
> Flames in the streams; in all the bushes, gods!
> The darkest tree a golden glow discloses!
> O Sun! Without thee, roses were . . . just roses;
>   And clods, just clods![6]

He has revealed to no one the deep secret of his task: in order for the Sun to rise, he must sing, and the more inspired his song, the more beautiful the dawn: "I sing clear that it may be clear! . . . If Dawn be gray, I have not sung aright."[7] Nevertheless, Chanticleer suffers from a great sense of insecurity concerning his extraordinary gift of song, and consternation over his role in the universal order of things:

> I made the Sun rise. How? And whence? And why?
> When reason comes again, a fool am I.
> . . . .
> I find myself unworthy of my gift.
> . . . .
> Can I be sure, if I but do my part,
> I'll find my song still welling from my heart?[8]

Not far from the barnyard, there is a splendid forest inhabited by thousands of birds that sing their gratitude to St. Francis. All the sylvan animals are happy—even the envious toads, who despise the Nightingale because his song is so beautiful compared to their croaking. A climate of rebellion now reigns in the forest, however, because here lives the Pheasant Hen, the flirt, the coquette, the bird of gold who identifies herself as the Golden Fleece, and whose beauty enthralls like that of the dawn.

The two principal domains are, then, the barnyard and the forest, but there is also the tea-garden, where the Guinea Hen lives. Whenever there is a social gathering in the garden, the guest list is always quite remarkable: artifically hatched chicks, two-headed animals, and a wild assortment of heteroclitical fowl. The master of ceremonies at these "tea-conferences," where Morality is discussed with great sophistication, is Peacock, the poseur. The tea-garden undoubtedly represents those artifically created social situations in which Rostand personally felt so uncomfortable. The hostess and her hypocritical guests lack the sincerity and warmth that Rostand so fervently sought and did not find in Paris' teacup-balancing circles.

Apart from the Blackbird and the Peacock, who refer to themselves as "moderns" and really do not wish to harm anyone, Chanticleer has some serious enemies among the Night Birds—those animals that meet every night on a lugubrious promontory to plot the assassination of the symbol of Light and Beauty. Their motto is "Shadow and Prey," and any reference to Dawn or Day makes them shudder:

> Long live the Night to vengeance given!
> When the tom-tit's heart is riven
> For his graces!
> Darkness is at war with Beauty.[9]

To eliminate Chanticleer means the liberation of the world of night and darkness. Chanticleer, therefore, must die. How he is to be put to death is an age-old problem, and every generation of screech-owls, horned owls, and cats discusses this timeless question with cruel ferocity. The Night Birds are clearly symbolic of those destructive forces that conspire to destroy the creative spirit in man.

One night a shot is heard. The magnificent Pheasant Hen, "gold-robed, daughter of kings," terrorized but proud, rushes from the forest to take refuge in Chanticleer's barnyard. Here begins the game of emotion that permits a psychological study of the main characters and that must be analyzed before discussing their symbolism, which is the principal interest of the play. The emotional game is divided, naturally, into acts. After his first amazement at finding himself in the company of a golden Pheasant Hen, Chanticleer then begins his famous "cocorico" of the Cock in love. The Pheasant Hen remains, however, quite unmoved; her feelings are simple and her response is straightforward:

> . . . I'm not susceptible; I'm not demure,
> And for my taste, the Cock is too cocksure.
> . . . And spoiled. The only mate I'd own
> Would love, not glory, but myself alone.[10]

After accompanying the Pheasant Hen on a tour of the barnyard, Chanticleer becomes confidential and reveals his passion for the Sun to her; but she is coquettish and indifferent to any passion that is not centered on herself. She goes off to the rendezvous of the Night Birds and meets the Blackbird who first makes fun of her fears, then hides when Chanticleer enters. The Pheasant Hen succeeds in drawing Chanticleer's secret from him: he makes "a glorious day to rise"! To the Pheasant Hen's inquiry: "You think your crow across the world is hurled?", Chanticleer replies with simplicity but conveys nobly and movingly Rostand's own philosophy:

> I don't know very well what is the world.
> I crow for this my Valley,—hoping, so
> In every valley, is one cock to crow.[11]

Responding to Chanticleer's fervor, the Pheasant Hen cries out: "He is so beautiful he may be right!"[12] Chanticleer has never sung better than on this morning, yet the Sun delays its appearance. Then comes the inevitable moment in which the Cock loses confidence in his singing, but the Pheasant Hen encourages him, exclaiming: ". . . My glorious Cock, you make / The sun to rise!"[13], as, indeed, it does. At this point, the Blackbird arrives on the scene. After first mocking Chanticleer, he then confides to him that a plot against his life is in the making. Chanticleer decides to leave for the Guinea Hen's social gathering, where he finds himself among a thousand splendid and eccentric beings. He is very confused and turns in despair to the Pheasant Hen who begs him to leave and go into the forest with her. She almost succeeds in persuading him, but Chanticleer draws back with a thwarted feeling: "No, I must sing where Fate decrees. / Here, I am useful and beloved."[14] Chanticleer knows he is loved by the Pheasant Hen, but he cannot retreat from his line of duty. His long tirade of puns and *cliquetis* on the word "cock" follows:

Cockarde, cock-feather, cock and cockalan,
With supercockly cockernonies crested, . . .
—I prate like Peacock when my wrath has bested
My silent resolution,—Cockatoos, cockaded
With coquelicos, cockerily shaded;
Not cocksure only of your cocoricos,
You are—just poppycock and hybrid echoes!
Fashion! the cock-brained victim that she chooses
For her cock-bree, just plays cock-all,—and loses!
She, cock-a-bendy, takes you cock-a-hoop,
Then throws you down, like chickens with the roup,
Like old cock-metal or last year's cocoon,
When some new cock with coccyx more buffoon
Comes cock-a-pentie 'gainst her cock-hedge rotten!
Well in a . . . cock-a-trice . . . he'll be forgotten!
Of all coqueluchons cockarde ever wore,
Some egg can hatch one cockaleekie more.
Cockchaffers chased, rococo cocks again
Will go eat cockles, exiled from Cockayne![15]

The only possible answer to such provocative words is the entrance of the formidable Fighting Cock, White Pile, who boasts of having killed, on his tour in both Americas, "three Clayborns, two Sherwoods, a brace of Smoks and a Black Sumatra," as well as "five Red Games at Cambridge and ten Braekel at Brussels."[16] White Pile now engages Chanticleer in a hideous and symbolic cock-fight at which the poultry spectators call for blood and death until Patou silences them by telling them they sound like men! White Pile reduces Chanticleer to an exhausted, bleeding, reeling mass but does not succeed in killing him. The shadow of the hawk falls over the scene. All are terrorized—except Chanticleer, who suddenly stands on his feet, at his full height, his wounds forgotten, and takes all the animals under his protection. Once the danger has passed, the battle with White Pile resumes, but Chanticleer seems to have acquired new energy after having protected the animals, and he forces his adversary to retreat from the battlefield. The Pheasant Hen is at the height of her joy, and Chanticleer sweetly announces that tomorrow the Sun will rise again. He does not succeed in singing, however, and with a cry of despair, he throws himself on the Pheasant Hen's breast. He can only say: "I love you! Let us flee!"

He has found love and admiration, but Chanticleer's personality has
not changed. He will remain the same old Cock, with the same
sense of duty.

In the strangely bewitched forest, Chanticleer is not completely
happy. Nor is the Pheasant Hen. She permits him to sing only one
song a day, for she is jealous of Light and Duty, which inspire such
passion in her lover. She seeks to divert Chanticleer's desire solely
toward herself:

> The dawn is pretty, true, but one must live.
> Oh you male creatures! Lacking hens, my dear,
> How often you'd be duped![17]

They argue. Chanticleer refuses to comply with the Pheasant Hen's
request that he remain one entire day without singing, and his
thoughts turn to his old home, the barnyard. He will hear the latest
news

> By telephone. The morning glory vine
> About his cage has roots that intertwine
> With this white bind-weed by the water, so
> We find the service pretty good.
> . . . .
> No other flower keeps open every night.[18]

The Pheasant Hen now undertakes to organize a forest conspiracy
in order to impose her will on Chanticleer. The toads try to convince him that the song of the Nightingale is ugly, but the eternal
song that vibrates through the forest so seduces and bewitches
Chanticleer that he says to the Nightingale, despairingly: "Oh,
sing! But, knowing crystal, shall I trust / My copper trumpet?"[19]
The Nightingale responds: "What does it matter! Sing, Ah sing!
though knowing / That nobler songs from other lips are flowing![20]
This exhortation to duty is interrupted by a detonation and a flash
of gunfire from the thicket. The song of the Nightingale is abruptly
silenced. The forest's "little André Chénier" is dead: "Yes, men are
strong / And they send bullets where they hear a song."[21] Chanticleer is heartbroken; the Pheasant Hen invites him to weep under
the shelter of her wings. She embraces him thus until dawn draws
near, then, almost gloatingly, cries out that dawn has come without

the song of the Cock! Chanticleer utters a cry of agony. The Pheasant Hen proclaims: "Better a heart pressed closer against your heart / Than the High Heaven that does its work apart!"[22] Chanticleer, however, springs away from her, stands at his full height, and, despite his shattered kingdom, cries out in a loud voice: "Cocorico!" Eyes must be opened! New, more melodious song bursts forth from the forest. Chanticleer is again convinced that he must sing—"sonorous, clear, exact"—and that other cocks must repeat the song in every common barnyard in order to dispel the Night.

Chanticleer then invites the Pheasant Hen to occupy second place in his heart, after the dawn. At her stubborn answer, "never," he sighs gently and adds with Cornelian firmness:

> . . . I adore you. Therefore I
> But ill could serve the Great Cause I adore,
> Near one who values any creature more![23]

and he disappears from her sight. There is a poacher in the area, however, and the owls in the treetops rejoice that the Cock is in danger. At this point, the Pheasant Hen, inspired by Chanticleer's nobility of purpose and magnanimity of soul, demontrates her own heroism. She flings herself into the peril in order to protect her beloved Chanticleer, but as she flies toward him, she is caught in a snare. Her only thought is that she cannot help her lover, and, terrorized by her hopelessness, she reveals her magnificent altruism:

> Oh, let him live! And I will find my share
> Of all the world within his barnyard there!
> O Sun, my Cock your banner has unfurled
> That makes his shadow . . . that makes all my world![24]

A detonation is heard; she utters a sharp cry; silence falls; then, from the far-off distance is heard the voice of Chanticleer: "Cocorico!" All the forest cries out: "Saved!", but the Woodpecker announces that the poachers are coming for the net in which the Pheasant Hen is ensnared. She closes her eyes in sacrifice, saying: "So be it, then." The curtain falls as Patou warns: "Men!" And in the net, wings spread wide, throat quavering, the Pheasant Hen senses the approach of the giant killer.

In *Chanticleer*, there are more naturally dramatic elements than
in *The Eaglet* or in *The Princess Far Away*. The action is more contemporary than that of *Romantics* or *The Woman of Samaria*. Like
Cyrano of Bergerac, it is more real, while at the same time it is
basically symbolic. Chanticleer and the struggle in which he is
engaged can be defined both realistically and symbolically. First of
all, it must be remembered that the Cock is not a "comic hero." He
is, Rostand affirms, "a bit of myself." Rostand, then, is the voice of
Chanticleer:

> I feel that I am needed and was born
> To be a trumpet and a curving horn.
> As sounding conch-shells speak with Ocean's voice,
> I am the Voice of Earth. And I rejoice
> To be not bird, not cock,—only a mighty cry,
> The cry of earth, uplifted to the sky!
> . . . .
> . . . My life and I
> Are only precious as we form a cry.[25]

What is the significance of the cry?

> This cry of earth, piercing the utmost night,
> Is such a cry of passion for the light,
> A cry of love so absolute, I say,
> For the fair treasure that we call the Day,
> . . . .
> The cry of Beasts, who need not to deceive,
> With naught to hide, nor any need to shrink;
> . . . .
> A cry of longing, love and need's distress
> For all of Beauty, all of Wholesomeness,
> Of all who wish in joy and Light of Day
> To do their work with none to say them nay.[26]

Recalling Cyrano's dream—"to be admirable, in all"—helps to il-
luminate Chanticleer's vision of the world in creation coming out of
the shadows, and conveys a sense of the sacred. A morning Cock is
always necessary, as is an evening Nightingale. For Rostand,
creative men are on this earth to perform their duty openly, joyfully, without interference from lesser forces which deflect the artist

from his sacred search for light and beauty. The planet's orchestration depends on men's simple and natural calls for Day, harmonized to form an indomitable force against Night.

The "cry of earth" is a cry for the humble, who believe in Light as long as they can see it. The night time is when it is beautiful—and difficult—to believe in Light. Chanticleer stands in the center of the antithesis between light and dark in his struggle with the Pheasant Hen. Every great singer, every great creator, has found himself at one time plunged into darkness and despair, locked in combat with the problems and difficulties of creating. During these moments, he finds himself in need of some form of support—love, for example. Love is a kiln for creative zeal. If this love is not understanding and sympathetic, however, or if it asks for all and is not willing to stand second in line after the duty of the creator toward his art, the creator finds himself torn by two passions, between two crosses. His energies are divided and his creative force weakened by the split. When the sense of duty is the stronger of the two passions, love succumbs in the struggle, but, dying, it communicates an important lesson to the poet; it gives him more perspective in his vision of duty. The love passion is thereby purified to the point of the most total abnegation (cf., "So be it, then."). The Pheasant Hen is the feminine figure who would like to earn for herself all the privileges and all the liberty that man has, while retaining the absolute right to dominate him through love, even to the detriment of his duty. The relationship in *Chanticleer* proves to be disastrous, since the character juxtaposed with the feminine figure is a poet. Like Roxane in *Cyrano of Bergerac*, the Pheasant Hen is the personification of love; they exert their strength and their influence on men and events; yet they are relegated to abnegation: the former to the convent, the latter to the poacher's nets.

Whereas, in *Cyrano of Bergerac*, Le Bret represented the positive spirit of common sense, the Blackbird in *Chanticleer* pushes common sense to its negative limit. He is everything that can be imagined as opposed to passion and idealism. At his side are the toads and the Night Birds, enemies of talent because they do not possess any themselves. They are envious because of their creative impotence. These are the real enemies of man, and it is not surprising that they are the same enemies against whom Cyrano was fighting. The hero of *Chanticleer* is a poet and essentially a man of action. He experiences the intoxication of genius through the success of his work; his dreams are of unlimited ambition; he attacks evil-doers, stupidity, and apathy; he suffers discouragement, disappointed desires, and loss of faith in himself. At first, love offers inspiration and consolation; but ultimately love serves to tyrannize the hero, to limit and even paralyze his work.

If a lesson must be drawn from *Chanticleer*, it is: "To sing, though knowing that nobler songs from other lips are flowing!" Dreams are necessary. The moral of the last scene of the play is that ". . . who loses the Great Dream / Must die, or rise and conquer in its beam!"[27] because effort and striving render noble and sacred even the most ignoble creature's performance. Can the bizarre animal figures in *Chanticleer* be taken seriously? Rostand had to make a choice between two approaches: either try to reconstruct an animal psychology, have his beasts speak as such, not have them say anything that would go beyond the limits of their assumed intelligence—an almost impossible task; or else treat his animals as symbols and have them speak as men. Having set out along the lines of the first approach, he perhaps was not able to resist the temptation of the second, and he went even beyond. Not content with giving his animals human sentiments, he endowed them with incredible literary knowledge. By so doing, he naturally put himself into a vulnerable position that facilitated attacks from the critics. The animals Rostand created are, indeed, too knowledgeable. To accept them and understand them, however, it is necessary to play the game. Were not Aristophanes' *Birds* so erudite that they could hold forth arguments on the organization of a Greek city? In the face of the indefinability of the animals, the problem of the *mise-en-scène* for *Chanticleer* assumed challenging proportions. Should the stage set attempt to depict an animal world, or should the characters be transposed on to the plane of the human world? Ripert affirms that the play, in fact, was and remains unstageable.[28]

When the reader or viewer is exposed to *Chanticleer* for the first time, he is struck by the brilliant dialogue, the rich plays on words, and, at times, by a freshness and verve in happy combination with impetuosity, enthusiasm, and satire. Rostand's contemporaries felt that the work harmed him as a dramatic author but enhanced his reputation as a poet.[29] Certainly, the lyric passages of the play are brilliant examples of French versification. There were even those who went so far as to proclaim that Rostand had caused the sun to rise over France.[30] The main defects of the work are found in the weak exposure of ideas. The play is too contrived, too far-fetched for presentation as a serious thesis work; and the language and style are too exaggerated. The plays on words—foreign and popular—and the affected metaphors are often disturbing when they lack taste and purpose. At the same time, however, there is much sincere and poetic lyricism in *Chanticleer*. The sonnets at the beginning of each act contain little jewels of expression. The invocation to the Sun, the ballads, and the dramatic, fast-paced dialogue of the Night Birds constitute examples of outstanding verse. Especially memorable is the scene in the forest under the moonlight, when the song of the Nightingale—romance without words and a succession of lost notes—causes sighs of ecstasy to arise from the heart of the forest. The conception of the entire work is a *tour de force*, but I personally can only reiterate the words of the Blackbird concerning *Chanticleer:* "I criticize details, admire [it] in block."

II   The Last Night of Don Juan:
The Winter of Rostand's Despair

Every year, at the beginning of November, on the day of the commemoration of the dead, Spanish theatrical companies interrupt their scheduled performances in theaters throughout Spain and present instead *Don Juan Tenorio*, a romantic drama by José Zorilla, written in 1844. Perhaps the reason for the choice of *Don Juan Tenorio* to celebrate All Souls' Day is motivated by the desire to stress the idea that death does not interrupt the correspondence of amorous sentiments between the living and the dead. Death, in fact, renders communication more efficacious, inasmuch as from their glorious place of repose the blessed souls of the dead can more effectively intervene on behalf of the beloved persons still living on earth.

The prototype of Don Juan goes back to ancient times. He is the cynical libertine whose life is at the service of his own insatiable amorous thirst. Acting symbolically as the diabolical power of the flesh, he treads on, crushes, and destroys all scruples, conscience, and morality. Haughty, bold, clever, generous, a perjurer and a

prodigal spender, Don Juan possesses all the arts of engaging conversation and seduction. He has supreme self-confidence, and there
is no woman—servant or queen—who can resist him. The Spanish
Don Juan, like Don Quixote or Celestina, is one of the most typical
creations of the national genius. He took shape in the splendid and
decadent *siglo de oro* (golden age), during which the rigidity of
Catholic morality brought changes in Spanish customs but did not
succeed in disguising the unbridled libertinage of the Spanish
nobility. The character of the Spanish Don Juan appears for the first
time in 1630, in the well-known work of Tirso de Molina, *El
Burlador de Sevilla*. Since his original creation, the figure of the
protagonist has evolved significantly in the course of successive
theatrical and nontheatrical renditions in Spain and elsewhere. Don
Juan has inspired the most diverse literary and musical geniuses of
Europe, such as Molière, Mozart, Goldoni, Byron, Dumas, Musset
and Shaw. He has become a universal myth which, although removed more or less from the original archetype, lives from one era to
the next in man's imagination. Notwithstanding his universality,
however, he remains, in his most genuine incarnation, a Spanish
hero—the most typical hero of the land dedicated to love and to the
mysteries of religion.

José Zorilla's drama differs notably from that of Tirso de Molina,
mainly because of the deeper sense of humanity which the former
lends to the hero. While in *El Burlador de Sevilla* Don Juan is an
unbridled *bon vivant*, completely deprived of any sentiments of
love, Zorilla's Don Juan reveals, with respect to his last victim, Doña
Iñes de Ulloa, an unexpected capacity for love, which saves him at
the very point of death. Zorilla's is a romanticized version of the
Don Juan myth and comes close to being a sacred representation or,
to use the Spanish term, an *auto sacremental.*[31] Its traditional form
helps to explain why Zorilla's drama finds such profound reper-
cussions in the hearts of the Spanish. Moreover, the distinctions
between sacred and profane are not so rigid as one would
believe—especially in Spain.

Don Juan Tenorio, written in verse in accordance with theatrical
tradition, is composed of seven acts (too many, by all critical stan-
dards), grouped into two distinct parts; there are four acts in the
first part, three in the second. The action takes place in Seville
around 1545, during the last years of the reign of Charles V. In the

first part, two young Seville noblemen, Don Juan Tenorio and Don Luis Mejìa, are concluding a contest in libertinage, which had begun as a result of an amorous misunderstanding. The contest ends with the victory of Don Juan Tenorio, who is able to boast a greater number of turpitudes: women deceived, betrayals, duels, assassinations. Don Juan, however, is not satisfied with the victory he has just won. Spurred on by his diabolic fury, he again challenges his friend and rival, Don Luis Mejìa, declaring himself ready to undertake two daring new enterprises: first, within six days, he will seduce from the convent a young lady of the nobility, Doña Iñes de Ulloa, who is about to take her vows; and, secondly, he will snatch away from Don Luis himself his fiancée, Doña Anna de Pantoja, who is just about to be led to the altar. The mad challenge is accepted, and Don Juan marks one point ahead in his two undertakings: Doña Iñes is conquered and kidnapped from the convent with the complicity of an intermediary. Subsequently, an infamous stratagem permits the conquest of Doña Anna de Pantoja. The encounter in the convent with Doña Iñes, however, has a surprise outcome: the dissolute seducer remains so struck by the innocence and virtue of his victim that he is disposed even to change his own life-style. He has caught a glimpse of the gates of heaven in the eyes of the young girl. Don Juan is no longer Don Juan. But Doña Iñes' father, Don Gonzalo, Commander of the Order of Calatrava, together with Don Luis, has decided to avenge the offended honor of the two women. Seeing himself thwarted in his bid for redemption, derided and mocked, Don Juan is obliged to seize his sword again and kill both of his persecutors. His flight from Seville follows: Doña Iñes dies of despair.

In the second part of the drama, Don Juan, pardoned by Charles V for his exceptional valor in battle, returns to his native land after five years and in Seville finds his mansion transformed into a burial vault in which repose the mortal remains of his victims: Don Gonzalo, Don Luis, and Doña Iñes. On each tomb stands a stone statue representing the deceased person. In the vault, the ghost of Doña Iñes speaks to her beloved and exhorts him to repent, mend his ways, and save himself from eternal damnation, assuring him that God will pardon him. Don Juan is moved, but since he does not believe in shades of the dead, he is convinced, in his presumptuousness, that he has suffered an attack of delirium. He reassumes his boldness and self-confidence to the point of turning to the statue of Don Gonzalo and inviting it to supper at his home. God accepts the impious provocation and allows the statue to appear in the dining room where Don Juan is having a banquet with his friends. Terrified, but not yet conquered, Don Juan accepts in turn Don Gonzalo's invitation to go to supper with him in the burial vault where the tombstone of the Commander of the Order of Calatrava has been transformed into an infernal banquet table. Among the dinner guests of skeletons and phantoms, Don Gonzalo announces Don Juan's imminent death. Only a few moments remain to him—scarcely enough time to repent for his crimes. The last grains of sand are flowing through the hour glass, and still Don Juan postpones his repentance. At the supreme instant, however, he falls to his knees, stretches his hand toward heaven, and asks pardon for his sins. The ghost of Doña Iñes grasps his hand and slowly leads her loved one on the path of salvation. Don Juan is redeemed through the miracle of love.

In Rostand's *The Last Night of Don Juan*, the poet cedes his place to the philosopher, permitting a detailed exposé of the author's ideas. The play is a more markedly symbolic work than the preceding ones, and, above all, it is an heroic work—the epitome of Rostand's thesis plays. If he had finished it, it might perhaps have proved to be his greatest contribution to the stage. What is most striking in the play is the variety of shadings of sadness and sobriety. No longer are felt the verve, the lyric heroism, and the meridional bravura of the preceding works. Rather, the feeling comes through that Rostand has lost his keen, buoyant enjoyment of life; that he is disillusioned by the critics and by the reception accorded his works. So he snuffs out his natural *joie de vivre* in order to be able to explain to the common mortals of this earth that "heaven is when one loves." Undoubtedly, Rostand felt that his health was failing and that he had to modify his conviction that the hero of the dream is the person in love. It was necessary to explain *what* love is. *The Last Night of Don Juan* offers abundant material for such an explanation.

In the Prologue of the play, Don Juan descends the stairway that leads to hell. He is impudent and shameless, but he has courage. The Statue of the Commander, which is leading him down the stairs, accords him a period of grace of ten years of life. Don Juan thereupon turns to go up the stairs again, reciting the names of his mistresses on each step. The First Part, ten years later, introduces Don Juan as a gay cavalier, thinking of his women and of his imminent death in Venice, the city of love. A Showman has set up a stage on which he presents a symbolic puppet show for Don Juan's benefit. When Punchinello sings

> I'm the famous Mignolet,
> Mighty general in the fray,
> Watch me make the ladies start![32]

Don Juan raises his drinking cup and sings:

> I'm the famous Burlador,
> At my belt are keys galore
> To unlock each lady's heart![33]

Part of his technique, he adds, is: "Don't beat a woman; make her suffer!"[34] and, says Don Juan, one must treat the Devil likewise. The latter appears to him under the guise of a marionette to ask him the reason for such a declaration. Don Juan answers:

> Well thou know'st
> The pain of holding over the abyss
> A dauntless soul! Thou lov'st to drag thy prey
> By the hair, the while he clings to every column!
> Thy horns, above the flame thy puffing fans,
> Like but to toss a conquered struggler. Me
> When thou hast taken, thou shalt not have *had!*[35]

The Showman then reveals that he is the Devil himself and demands the soul of Don Juan, since the ten-year period of grace has come to an end. While they are waiting to leave on the final journey, they sit down to talk and Don Juan relates the techniques of his art of seduction. In the course of the conversation, Don Juan declares that he prefers the Devil attired in green, because that is how he saw him dressed in Eden, when he was Adam, and Eve was beside him—in a dream. He boasts:

> . . . 'tis I myself
> That have possessed!
>
> . . . .
> Possession's knowledge! Knowledge! Understanding!
> I grasped their naked souls.[36]

In fact, Don Juan has a list of one thousand and three women that he has possessed—a list that he now tears up because he knows it by heart. The bits of torn paper flutter from a window, descending slowly into the Adriatic, and then return in the form of gondolas. From the gondolas disembark one thousand and three masked ghosts, each carrying a rose and a fan, and draped in a cloak that covers only spirit—no flesh! The Devil invites Don Juan to try to recognize and identify any one of the souls. If he succeeds, her mask will fall. Don Juan attempts to identify his past mistresses, but the souls, one after another, respond "no!" to the names he assigns them. He does not recognize them because the souls reveal "the gaze they showed when they were all alone."[37] Don Juan, upset but still full of self-confidence, lights a torch to seek out one he recognizes . . . and the curtain falls slowly. Why just at this moment? The explanation is philosophical rather than dramatic. Rostand is asking all of us: Can we know?

The Second Part of the play contains his answer: "All alone I stand / 'Mid souls, as in a forest."[38] Don Juan earlier had declared that he has "possessed." What do the Ghosts say?

> . . . woman knows,
> When man has giv'n the hint, what sort of lie
> He wishes her to yield with![39]

Don Juan protests that it was *he* who dominated, he who corrupted, he who seduced, and he who pleased the women. The Ghosts answer that he had simply dictated their own desires, and the Devil adds mockingly: " 'Watch me seduce the magnet!' says the iron."[40] Don Juan is now left with the sole consolation that at least he made women suffer. For Rostand, this concept is important, because for him suffering is considered noble and sacred. The Devil takes a goblet to gather all the tears that have ever been shed for Don Juan. He searches in the goblet for a sincere teardrop, but they are all false! Finally, he finds a real one: it is the tear of the White Ghost, who wept out of pity, not for herself, but for Don Juan. The spirit and the soul of the White Ghost are reflections of a pure, noble, and anguished heart. Don Juan cannot remember the name of this woman who symbolizes sincerity and true love—even after she whispers it into his ear! She drops her mask; he does not even recognize her face. The Devil holds out a copy of his torn list to Don Juan, but the name of this woman is the only one missing. Don Juan says:

> . . . need I be
> Downcast, because, out of a thousand times
> and four, I missed love but once?[41]

The White Ghost disappears then reappears immediately with the other Ghosts:

> . . .—in each
> Thou couldst have found me with a little love!
> . . . .
> In all I waited,
> And saw thee always passing by. Our hearts
> Beat for a listening ear alone, but thou
> Didst rest on them unhearing. Each of us
> Might have perhaps become the perfect mate,
> Hadst thou but tried— . . .[42]

The White Ghost maintains that as long as a flame continues to burn within her tear, Don Juan may still hope to find himself a heart. The Devil invites him to search, but adds that, if he learns to love, Don Juan will have vanquished the Devil. Don Juan tries to offer himself unto love, but at this point all the ghosts unmask, and he sees their faces which

> All have lied to me, so each
> Is therefore new! No, I have no more heart
> For one, while a new face intrigues me!
>
> . . . .
>
> . . . Woman was after all
> A pretext, nothing more! No, triumph not!
> I took you but to leap above myself
> To something higher. . . .[43]

This is Don Juan's sole triumph.

It is the Ghosts, however, who conclude the work. They ask Don Juan what has become of all the stimulation and exaltation they had produced in him. The White Ghost asks him what he has fashioned with her tear. To understand the moral of the play, it would suffice to imagine how Cyrano would have answered these questions had they been put to him. The Eaglet lacked passion for action and failed in action. Don Juan is a hero, in the sense of action, but he has failed in the creation: he has not succeeded in finding his heart. The Ghosts press him to consider that his past conquests have left him in possession of nothing. They urge him to repent, but Don Juan is firm:

> Not in the least do I repent!—Don Juan
> Is John of Austria, victor of Lepanto!—
> When death's at hand, wherefore does memory crave
> One deed to bind us to the future?—Nay,
> I'll not repent!—What are these searing flames?—
> Art thou Life's lover, Death, that thou dost plot
> Her vengeance? Must the fallen runner die,
> Burned by the torch he failed to pass along?[44]

The Devil attempts to drag him down to hell with him:

> Come, come along now! Thou art one of those
> Of whom no trace is left—no word remains,
> No gesture![45]

Even the Beggar, to whom Don Juan had given a gold coin "for the love of humanity," throws the coin in Don Juan's face with the words: "I'll strangle thee, for having dared to soil / Words that should feed our hope!"[46] Don Juan is now damned—which allows his soul to begin to shine through. He cries out:

> I long to suffer!
> I've never suffered! I've a right to hell!
> I've earned my hell![47]

But the Devil has already chosen Don Juan's form of hell: he is to be "damned within a puppet." Defiant, Don Juan replies that he will mock his hell by singing: "I'm the famous Burlador" and by beating the other puppets with a stick. The White Ghost weeps at the sight of Don Juan—"fit to wield a mighty sword"—and now reduced to a stick-swinging puppet.

What irony! Rostand believed that the theater is one of the greatest and most sacrosanct forces in society. But what is it in reality? It is the place where men and women run to enjoy Don Juan's hell. Don Juan is their real hero; through him they experience the primordial Adam and the eternal Eve, the serpent and the flesh with no veil covering it. "Ah, what a shame!" are the last words in the play. They fall from the lips of the White Ghost, with infinite despair.

CHAPTER 6

Conclusion

IT has been said that "when a writer states clearly that
one of his plays is symbolic, or if he has his characters express
philosophical ideas, and when he writes in verse, he is called a poet-
philosopher."[1] Rostand has stated clearly that *Chanticleer* is symbolic; many of his characters do express philosophical ideas, as has
been seen especially in *The Princess Far Away, Cyrano of Bergerac,*
and *The Last Night of Don Juan;* and he does write in verse, some
of which is the finest in French poetry. Rostand, the would-be poet-
philosopher, however, is always more of a poet than a philosopher.
He interprets the human experience and conceives his dramatic
oeuvre from a lyrical and spiritual rather than from a rational point
of view. His speech of acceptance on the day he took his seat in the
French Academy (June 4, 1903) clearly indicates that the dramatist
felt poetry to be the bridge between stage characters and audience:

Now there is scarcely any place, except in the theater, where souls, side by
side, can feel each others' wings . . . The characters of a play are the go-
betweens whose task it is to get us out of the eternal boarding school that
life is—get us out so that we may find the courage to go back in,
and . . . the one who best succeeds in getting us out is a hero![2]

I *Ideas*

The best understanding of Rostand's dramatic ideas, then, is
achieved through comprehension of the hero and heroic fervor in
the face of life's challenges and vicissitudes. The most heroic of
Rostandian heroes are, certainly, Cyrano, Chanticleer, and Joffroy
Rudel, but the "eternal boarding school" of which the author
speaks has been observed in a variety of settings. The garden of
Romantics is the life that Percinet and Sylvette had to get out of in

112

order to find the courage to go back in. Tripoli at the time of the Crusades *(The Princess Far Away)*, the time of Jesus Christ's teachings *(The Woman of Samaria)*, France in 1640 *(Cyrano of Bergerac)*, nineteenth-century Austria *(The Eaglet)*, the wide open countryside *(Chanticleer)*—all constitute some aspect of human life in routine, mediocre and rarely heroic times. Living their daily lives, Rostand's heroes experience joy and sorrow, they conquer or they pardon, but in each struggle they gain something important: a broader perspective, which adds a new dimension to human existence and renders life nobler and sweeter. Life is a sort of school if within its walls are taught the great lessons of human values. Those who have best learned these lessons are those who are able to go out into the world equipped with a sensitivity that allows them to gain possession of the vital warmth called love. Without it, the cold outside world brings death through spiritual inanition.

The reality of life for Rostand, the poet, is the dream. In *Romantics*, the dream is love, but before they reach a full understanding of it, the protagonists try to get out of life more than it can give, and they are therefore discontent. The dream in *The Princess Far Away* is incarnated in Melissinde, who symbolizes love. Here the dream has an almost supernatural power, and the Princess' lesser passion for Bertrand is, in the end, repressed by the sacrifice to a more sacred duty toward the dying Joffroy Rudel. In *Cyrano of Bergerac*, there is a double dream that corresponds to the double life of Cyrano himself. There is the dream of everyday life, and the dream of personal love. Cyrano's dream is to be extraordinary in everything; his every gesture, every action, is filled with bravura; but Rostand wishes to convey the realization that grace and gentleness can lie hidden in the dream: "*panache* is often in the sacrifice that we make . . . ." Suffering gives perspective to Cyrano's dream; sorrow enhances his character. This is clearly seen also in Chanticleer, whose dream it is to make the sun rise, thereby producing beauty, joy, health, warmth, and affection. His dream is so important and so sincere that, even after he is disabused, he protests that whoever loses the great dream must die, or rise and conquer. In *The Woman of Samaria*, there unfolds a dream that has enthralled the entire Christian world since the birth of Christ: the Gospel. The strength of this dream of feeling and action lies in the fact that, like all of Rostand's dreams, it is nourished by life itself.

Jesus succeeds in converting the people of Samaria by inspiring Photine with a living dream, whereas the Eaglet fails because he is incapable of making his dream live in himself and in others. Don Juan's mad desires provide no veils to cover his flesh; his goal is pursued with negative fervor and passion, which leave him with nothing but the emptiness of a puppet in the end. To each his dream—love, duty, *panache*, altruism, or even the naïve dream of the Eaglet, but a dream not supported by fervent zeal and enthusiasm leads to nothingness. Cyrano is zealous to the extreme, whereas the Eaglet's fervor may be looked upon as sentimental lyricism, completely introverted, not active, and therefore purposeless. Don Juan is zealous, but he does not dream. "What is life without a dream?" sings Joffroy Rudel.

Zeal, then, for Rostand, is that joyful energy that flows from the cultivation of a noble dream. The moving force of the dream renders it efficacious, but, at the same time, the additional element of love needs to be added. A certain personal warmth and a certain earthly passion play a crucial role in Rostand's plays, even the one revolving around the divine figure of Jesus. Earthly love is the foundation of the Rostandian dream. Love must be taken seriously. Romantic, affected love, however, does not last; the only real, true love is based on free will, which inspires great sacrifices; it is the love that lends heroic warmth to the dream. If it is the dream that renders the hero's life meaningful, it is his own zeal that renders it sacred, love renders it noble, and poetry renders it beautiful and good. Rostand offers an appropriate definition of poetry:

It is without doubt the veil that envelops the flesh; it is a halo which the poet casts around ordinary life in order to ennoble it, embellish it, poeticize it. . . . It is the joy of living, expressed in song.[3]

Rostand's poetry is certainly affected, but his sincerity saves it from artificiality. It is sincerity as one of the most important human values that the author attempts to communicate through his plays. The discovery of sincerity renders the life of Sylvette and Percinet in *Romantics* spontaneous and happy; Cyrano fights for sincerity, especially in matters of friendship and love; the sincerity of the Eaglet is one of the causes of his tragedy; Chanticleer shies away from the Blackbird because he lacks candor; and, finally, it is sincerity that the White Ghost is seeking in Don Juan.

These are Rostand's ideas in their broadest lines. Do they constitute a philosophy?

No, because they do not give us any answers to the important questions concerning human destiny or our *raison d'être*. Is Rostand, then, a poet-philosopher? Again no, because he does not take the facts of existence and order them into a system of values that might constitute a universe.[4]

The total effect of Rostand's theater does not have the impact of a philosophical idea; it produces, however, more than a simple feeling; it comes close to achieving the "quality of a prayer,"[5] and this is the basis of Rostand's artistic concept. He seeks to represent a significant idea through a lyric, sentimental gesture, as well as to create a personal prayer for each one of us, regardless of the times in which we live.

With regard to his choice of historic times and places, it must be remembered that Rostand has interpreted history as a poet and as a prophet, and not as an historian. His lessons are for the soul; they are not representations of the past for the mind of the chronicler. The past does, in fact, spring alive in his works, but it is thanks to his profound observation of the human heart and not to his historic erudition. Moreover, he defended himself against possible reproaches for not having respected historical accuracy by declaring that even when the poet is wrong, he is right.

II *Plot Construction*

As for plot construction, Rostand, as has been mentioned, was the outstanding student in his composition class at the Collège Stanislas. Yet some critics have reproached him "for having composed his plays so badly."[6] By judging his plays as intellectual or heroic works, however, these critics have lost sight of the fact that Rostand wanted to provide lessons for the soul; it is to the soul and not to the orderly mind that he addresses himself invariably. The acts of the play are the preparation and instruction of the soul, the final lesson, and a conclusion that is both moral and poetic. Such is Rostand's dramatic procedure, even though, at times, the action drags and the secondary plots take the upper hand. In *Romantics*, for example, the last two acts are not strictly necessary; in *The Princess Far Away*, the last act is superfluous, as it is in *The Woman of Samaria*. With regard to the masterpieces, it should be pointed out that Rostand does not use the first act to "pose the question," and, in *Chanticleer*, the first act does not lead logically to the end of the work; it is necessary to wait until the end of the second act for the statement of the situation. As one critic has written:

> . . . the composition of the plays is rather weak from the point of view of logical, unifying action; there is even, truthfully speaking, a certain lack of originality in the conceiving of plots; that is, Rostand seems to be quite satisfied using worn out material; finally, one is unable to discern, at first glance, any unity in his artistic work. But . . . unity is found in the personal, active, heroic and romantic lyricism of the sentiments, so his plays resemble epic poems rather than plays. . . . Their interest lies not in their psychology nor their intelligence: one must seek their interest rather in the essentially human feeling of the soul.[7]

III   *Style*

Rostand's style may now be examined in the light of his ideas. It is a style made up of images—images of heroic action, of things poetic, of color, music, and even perfumes. Somewhat affected and exaggerated at times, the images are nevertheless highly original and unforgettably Rostandian. Consider the following purely descriptive images: "But not too much of '89, I beg, / For pressure has been known to break an egg;"[8] "To hold Orestes bounden as with chains, / While his Pylades dies, he knows,—and he remains!"[9] To Chanticleer's inquiry whether she comes from the East, whence comes the Dawn, the Pheasant Hen replies: "My life is full of picturesque disorder / —If from the East, from the Bohemian border."[10] Other images from *Chanticleer:* "How well she fits her clothes . . . ; they might as well / Wear smocks, those other [hens] there;[11] "A bumblebee with burly noise and furs / Knocks at a lily's door;[12] and:

> Those popinjays, convulsed, deformed, uncouth,
> Have neither style nor beauty, line nor truth.
> Their forms have lost the egg-shell's sweet ellipse.
> —A poultry yard from the Apocalypse![13]

The dying Cyrano, referring to Roxane's beauty, says expressively:

"One soft gown brushed my path before the end."[14] When the two families in *Romantics* are reconciled, Bergamin declaims:

> Hate dies at Hymen's altar. Love is all.
> Peace is made.
> (*He points dramatically to the wall.*)
>   The Pyrenees must fall.[15]

An onlooker describing the Samaritan crowd, motionless in the presence of Jesus, says: " 'Tis like a lion whose enormous paw / Scarce dares to hold the snowy lamb it felled."[16] Cyrano, threatening to slay the entire audience at the Montfleury performance, to a citizen's: "Aha, Has Samson come?" retorts "To make the test, lend me your jaw-bone, friend;" then, turning to the obese actor whose performance he has banned, he announces: "I shall clap thrice, Full Moon. / When I have done, Eclipse yourself."[17]

Even Rostand's philosophy is expressed in images. The following are some images of action: "One man who walks among you still prefers / Music of ringing truth to ringing spurs."[18]; "You will lose the crown that is to-night so near / If you go back! / If I go forward, I will lose my soul!"[19]; "A living Wagram always in your sight!"[20]; "A crystal shattered by a bell of bronze!"[21] The poet conceived action not only in concrete images, but also in color and music. He loved colors—especially white, gold, red and blue. The white sail in *The Princess Far Away* is seen by Melissinde as:

> White under the blue heaven!
> White as the hope of pardon! God! Forgive!
> Prolong, dear God, this whiteness seen afar,
> For that white sail becomes my highest star![22]

Photine, speaking of Christ's white soul, says: "White shadows on my soul from His soul fell."[23] Other examples of color images are the following: "Wagram, all white a willing offering stands."[24]; "Hands; cold hands, so white, so still! / Sad hands that miss one golden circlet still!"[25] Chanticleer's five-stanza apostrophe to the Sun in Act I, scene 2, is an audio-visual symphony in gold. A burst of contrasting colors characterizes Bertrand's description of the eyes of Joffroy Rudel's inaccessible Princess:

> His bitter pains were clean forgot I trow,
> If he behold the whiteness of her brow,—
> If he behold, beneath the tawny lashes
> The blue eyes, that are gray, where emerald flashes![26]

The Pigeon, describing the effect of Chanticleer's crowing, dips into his palette of colors with artistry:

> It adds a nobler beauty to the scene
> Than a white hamlet to a mountain's green.
>
> . . . .
>
> Pierces the azures like a ray of light,—
> A golden needle with a thread of gold
> Joining the sky and valley fold on fold![27]

On the morning that Chanticleer and the Pheasant Hen declare their love, a spectrum of colors replaces the fading night:

> PHEASANT: The blue has lost its gloom!
> CHANTICLEER: Now it is green
> PHEASANT: Green, orange!
> CHANTICLEER: Green turned to gold
>   You are the first, this morning, to behold!
> PHEASANT: The dawn seems bounded by the purple heather!
>   . . . Oh, Yellow in the pines!
> CHANTICLEER: All must be gold together![28]

Rostand, as a man of the theater, used all kinds of stage effects and, as a background for the action, added the "gesture" in the form of a painting or a color to awaken the senses, with music as a poetic accompaniment. First, there is the music and sound of the descriptive images, then the music of the verses, and, finally, the use of pleasing and diverting sound effects. Some short examples are: "Play to them, . . . country airs, . . . the soft notes falling / Like little sisters' voices, calling, calling;"[29] ". . . the Dawn! / An evil word to hatch! / It grates as grates the striking of a match!"[30]; "And thou, Saint Francis, blesser of our wings, / Pray for us!"[31] The repetition of the s sound in this last verse conveys the whispered murmurings of the birds at prayer in *Chanticleer*. The wanton woman of Samaria, experiencing Jesus' love, receives Him as living water: "Gush, Spring of Love, and mount in jets of faith / And fall in drops of hope, dispelling death."[32] An onomatopoetic *tour de force*, combining nature and psyche, is contained in the far-away Princess' hazy spiritual dream:

> Yes, in my garden gleaming mistily,
> I hear the wind in myrtle trees repining;
> I sail o'er Syrtes' waters supple, shining,
> Where my proud galley, carven, gold-bedight,
> Mirrors its flowers by day, its gleams, by night,
> And my soft lute, buoyed by the plectrum's chords,
> Inspires my verses and the wave accords.
> Or in these halls, in solitude's completeness,
> My soul grows sad,—and sorrow has its sweetness!
> Here where my lilies press, on pave and plinth,
> My dream leads through a misty labyrinth;
> Little by little, leads to paths supernal;
> Reason sleeps in the tinkle sempiternal. . . .[33]

Among the Rostandian images that convey a feeling of eternity and spirituality even while stimulating the senses may be cited, from *Chanticleer*, the Nightingale's "I feel, all little, lost in this black tree, / The mighty soul of evening stirs in me;"[34] as well as Cyrano's "Winds from the past have given me strength to prove / My courage . . ."[35] and, from *The Woman of Samaria:*

> . . . the angels who today look on,
> Will feed your hunger with their wide-spread wings,
> Assuage your thirst with harps of myriad strings.
> By winds and harmonies the soul is fed.[36]

Other passages worth quoting in this category of images are:

> She who had been so kind a breath ago!
> I was as one deluded, one who dreamed.
> On the deserted air, a fragrance streamed,
> Light witness, as your floating veil fled by,
> Like to the perfumes, drifting ceaselessly,
> That will haunt Tarsus to the very last.
> Because once that way Cleopatra passed.[37]

From *The Eaglet:*

> . . . my father
> Through whose hands all a firmament has passed
> Has surely left his son this much at last,—
> Some star dust from his Star. . . .[38]

The preceding analysis of images contributes to an evaluation of Rostand's poetic genius as manifesting itself particularly in settings that appeal to the senses. For his stylistic imagery he uses all the physical aspects of a scene, even down to perfumes and taste, thus arousing the spectator's or reader's sensibilities and emotions. The technique lends the essence of prayer to Rostand's works.

The movement of the poetry remains to be examined, inasmuch as the rhythm of Rostand's verses is as varied as the works themselves. He uses every rhetorical device to create new tempos: hiatus, interjection, onomatopaeia, and literary *tour de force* that sometimes is so exaggerated that it becomes arrhythmic and prosaic. Examples are one of his verses, in the French text, which is composed of only two cacaphonic words: "Kaléidoscopiquement cosmopolite!" and the following verses of the Peacock in *Chanticleer:*

> Recall dodecagynia most amethyst,
> They're less cuproid, prasine and smaragdine
> Those multiform fires that we often have seen
> Which rain from all skies, most fourteenth-of-Julyly;
> Capital capitules capitularily.[39]

Moreover, the extended play on the word "cock," combined with innumerable alliterations and assonances of the sounds in "cocorico" in the third act of *Chanticleer,* produce a somewhat tedious cacaphony.

To produce his kaleidoscopic verbal effects, especially in *Cyrano of Bergerac* and in *Chanticleer,* Rostand uses words of every sort: rare, archaic, foreign, dialect, and an abundance of proper names. An illustration of the striking use of proper names to create a dizzying effect are the following lines from *Cyrano of Bergerac:*

> Baron of Peyrescous of Colignac.
> . . . .

> Of Casterac of Cahuzac,
> Vidame of Malgouvre of Escarabiot,—
> Chevalier of Antignac, Baron Hillot
> Of Castel-Crabioules of Salechan. . . .[40]

Patricia Williams writes:

Rostand employs a number of somewhat uncommon words such as colichemardes, délabyrinthez, escogriffes, estafilades, icosaedre, naisigère, pentacrostiche, pharaminieux, tryanneau. Moreoever he appears to have invented at least two words: hippocampelaphantocamelos and regromontanus. The use of these pedantic and amusing words appropriately serves to support the précieux quality of the play. It seems therefore apparent that the language of *Cyrano de Bergerac* effectively sustains dramatic tension, reveals characters and themes.[41]

Rostand excels in communicating the rhythm of crowds, especially in the scene in the city of Sichem, where the rhythmic eloquence of Photine is locked in a struggle against the hostile arrhythmia of the townspeople. Memorable, too, is the rhythm of the forest in *Chanticleer*, with the song of the Nightingale and the fascinating tempo of the animal choruses. If Rostand's originality in conceiving plots is not very striking and if his character studies are rather vague, the poetic ensemble of his style, imagery, and theatrical verse, on the other hand, render his work incomparable. His artistry with rhymes as well as with words is undisputable:

A poet, yes; but a writer, no. He is a prodigious adventure, a momentary reality, a unique "case."[42]

IV   Influences on Rostand

Although he is undoubtedly an exceptional literary case, an attempt will be made here to discover what influences determined Rostand's style. He is certainly a Romantic poet, because his work is inspired by personal emotion which is shared by the sensitive reader. Moreover, his is a dramatic production rich in all the old tricks of the Romantic theater: antitheses, incognitos, cape and sword, etc. *Romantics* is a gracious, delicate comedy modeled on the plays of Alfred de Musset. Victor Hugo had always been Rostand's self-appointed master. Both poets felt the importance of their mission; both used sonorous phrases. There is, however, an element in Rostand's theater that is not typical of the Romantic school: preciosity. Two kinds of preciosity—sincere and ridiculous—are present in all of his works. The latter kind is noticeable in *Romantics, Cyrano of Bergerac,* and *Chanticleer.* The former is noticeable everywhere. It is a preciosity of dramatic images and therefore not seventeenth-century preciosity which is cerebral and of a porcelain beauty. What is most interesting, however, is that in Rostand's precious poetry, the accent falls neither on the idea nor on the beautiful, but rather on the action. Rostandian preciosity is a means of expressing what for him is important in life—that is, zealous action.

To pinpoint the various influences on Rostand's style would be a boundless task.

The reason is that Rostand is a Provençal but he is a man of the theatre; he is a literary artist, but a preacher of ideas; he is a *précieux* troubadour but at the same time an epic dramatist. So it is easy to catch in every great artist a glimpse of what might have influenced Rostand's genius: there is the lyric and imaginative amplitude of Shakespeare; there are the comedies of Corneille—a sort of heroic comedy; there is the impetuosity (but not the psychology) of Racine's passion-love; there is the wit and amusing verve of Regnard; there are the refined delicacies of marivaudage; there are the *coups de théâtre* and the intrigues of Beaumarchais; there is the vagabond fantasy of Banville; . . . there is the exaltation of youth, the imagination and sensitivity of lyric tirades which remind us of Musset's comedies; but undoubtedly Rostand, as he himself confessed, is the continuation of Hugo.[43]

Hugo, however, is emphatic and resounds eloquently; Rostand consents to being great through simplicity alone.

V   *Rostand's Influence*

Edmond Rostand appeared on the French literary scene during an era of boredom and disenchantment, when there were no practical or precise goals to be achieved, either in literature or in art. The leaden, gray sky over France prompted him to rekindle the sun; and the lack of direction among his contemporaries inspired him to offer heroic visions and examples of meaningful action.

Above all, Rostand tried to reawaken in Frenchmen's souls that deep sentimentality that had existed in the past and was all too quickly disappearing from France's life-style. His efforts have been well described:

This sweet and profound sentimentality spread throughout all of his works, this resigned and penetrating melancholy, this valiant and exuberant gayety, which nourishes and fortifies itself . . . and finds in its outbursts of laughter new pretexts for laughter, this shrewd, mocking, maliciously friendly spirit: that is Rostand's sentimentality, his melancholy, his gayety, his spirit. Let's add to all that his great sincerity, which increases the force of heroic impulse toward noble and beautiful action; and we see what Rostand attempted to do.[44]

Rostand's moral influence was best felt in 1914 when young Frenchmen left for the battlefront to repel the German invasion. Some of them created a "Cyrano" division and adopted as their insignia the cock, Chanticleer. One of Rostand's poems, "Le Nom sur la Maison," ("The Name on the House") inspired an opera by the same name. Oddly enough, the opera glorifies the family, the cult of the domestic hearth, and national rebirth, just at a time when a generation of young Frenchmen was turning to André Gide, who had proclaimed his revolt against the family and had written: "I do not want to remember . . . I do not believe in dead things . . . I do not want to look back."[45]

The influence of Rostand was destined to be shortlived, however, both because of his art and because of his ideals. His triumph as a writer of heroic comedy was undercut by the fact that there is nothing essentially original in his work. His characters do not have faces; they are verbal fabrications. In *Romantics*, Rostand seems to be parodying himself because he knows Musset's influence is so obvious. His contemporaries graciously accepted the parody, the pseudo-Romanticism and the contrived refinement of the plot, the characters, and the alexandrine verses. Rostand was less cautious in *The Princess Far Away:* his second-hand narration of the legend of the troubadour, Joffroy Rudel, suffers from the fact that he destroyed its lyric simplicity by rendering it dramatic. The plot becomes complicated; a betrayal is added; and no fewer than twenty-four characters, plus the supernumeraries, sustain the situation for four long acts. The beautifully rhymed ballad contained in

the play is unforgettable — but might have been written by a Hugo
or a Banville. The Rostandian style lent itself poorly to the Gospel
according to Saint John for *The Woman of Samaria*. Jesus' entrance
on stage is too melodramatic; he is too gallant; the verses he recites
clash with the traditional concept of Christ. *Cyrano*, however,
redeemed Rostand for the error of judgment he had made in writing
the Biblical play. The Parisian public, thirsty for an ideal, for fantasy, for the colorful and the implausible, after ten years of
bourgeois realism in the theater, breathed a sign of relief and lived
vicariously and joyously in their swashbuckling swordsman. *The
Eaglet*, however, was a subsequent disappointment, for there was
no reason for Napoleon's son, Metternich, and Maria Luisa to speak
the language of Cyrano. The six long acts of *The Eaglet* are dis-
connected episodes, and dramatic construction is almost completely
lacking in the play. Rostand then turned to a setting that he felt
would better serve his stylistic purposes—nature and the animal
world. The human parody failed to interest the public, which
seemed to prefer Rostand's melodramatics to his preciosity. After
the failure of *Chanticleer*, Rostand turned away from the theater
and poured his bitterness into *The Last Night of Don Juan*.

Yet, despite many artistic and idealistic shortcomings, Rostand's
lyricism and romanticism are striking and have their effect even today. Many of his thoughts touch the chords of our purest and
deepest sentiments; many of his reflections take us back in time, incite us to evaluate our very existence, and force us to make comparisons between our life and the one of which the poet sings. The
most forceful work, in this respect, is undoubtedly *Cyrano of
Bergerac*; but there are many thought-provoking verses in *The
Eaglet* and in fragments of *Chanticleer* and *The Last Night of Don
Juan*. To undergo the influence of Rostand's works, however, we
must approach them in a particular frame of mind and free of our
social and intellectual masks. We must be willing to recognize
ourselves in the heart of the poet; we must sense that he was expressing himself perfectly in his great verses and we must share his
enthusiasm. Only those of us who have really experienced the
sadness of an equivocal love and the ineffable serenity that comes
from knowing that we have been able to give happiness to another
person—gratuitously—can understand Cyrano's mind, his exquisite
poetry, and his splendid, noble soul. As for Chanticleer, we must,

like him, be aware that we are pursuing an ideal, we must be certain of the utility of our existence and of our capacity to put other people's happiness above our own. We must have the knowledge that we are singing "though knowing that nobler songs from other lips are flowing." These are the prerequisites that can prepare us to enjoy and love Rostand's symbolic cock. *The Last Night of Don Juan* is conducive to reflection on our human existence, on how much truth and purity we have allowed to shine through during our short terrestrial stay. Have we been able to love sincerely—and sufficiently—to provoke the shedding of a real tear from the eyes of those whom we profess to love? Or has our life been just a show, and shall we, too, be condemned to the "eternal theatre?"

Reading Rostand's work is a bit like going in search of things past. It forces an evaluation of our actions and our feelings. Rostand's greatness lies in his mood descriptions, and he has an exceptional capacity for inviting us to meditate on certain phrases that sound like prayers so that we may learn to give *feeling* its just value, to topple *reason* off its pedestal—or, at least, to re-dimension it with respect to the total meaning of life. Serenity, if not happiness, might reign. Let us be iconoclasts by rejecting selfishness as our idol. Perhaps this is Rostand's dedicatory message to us all.

Notes and References

Preface

1. Cf. Louis Haugmard, *Edmond Rostand* (Paris: Sansot & Co., 1910), *passim*.

Chapter One

1. Elly Katz, *L'Esprit français dans le théâtre d'Edmond Rostand* (Toulouse, 1934), *passim*.

2. The word will be used frequently throughout this book to mean "heroic flourish of manner; flamboyance." In *Cyrano of Bergerac*, it retains its meaning of an ornamental military plume. Adolphe Cohn defines *le panache* as "an external quality which adds colour and brilliancy to internal things already worth having for their intrinsic value. Its main justification is personal bravery." (*Cyrano de Bergerac*, translated from the French by Charles Renauld, with an introduction by Adolphe Cohn [New York, 1899], p. vi).

3. *Les Musardises* (Paris, 1922), p. 193.

4. M. Rageot, cited in J. W. Grieve, *L'Oeuvre dramatique d'Edmond Rostand* (Paris, 1931), p. 15.

5. Cited in J. W. Grieve, *op. cit.*, p. 15.

6. *Les Musardises, op. cit.*, p. viii.

7. Emile Ripert, *Edmond Rostand* (Paris, 1968), p. 16.

Chapter Two

1. Cambo-les-Bains is a small spa in the Basses-Pyrénées, *arrondissement* of Bayonne, where there now exists an Edmond Rostand museum.

2. Rostand's poem is highly reminiscent of Baudelaire's "L'Albatros" on the same subject.

3. *Les Musardises, op. cit.*, p. 13.

4. The sonnet was recited by the author on December 9, 1896, from the stage of the Théâtre de la Renaissance, in homage to Sarah Bernhardt.

5. Rostand recited this poem in the students' presence at a matinee performance of *Cyrano of Bergerac* at the Théâtre de la Porte Saint-Martin on March 3, 1898.

6. Jules Renard (1864 - 1910) was a Realist writer, best known for his novel *Poil de carotte*.

Chapter Three

1. *Plays of Edmond Rostand,* translated by Henderson D. Norman (New York, 1921).

2. Translated by Mary Hendee (New York: Doubleday and McClure Co., 1899); and by Barrett H. Clark (New York: Samuel French, 1915).

3. Norman, *op. cit., Romantics,* I, 9, p. 20.

4. *Ibid.,* III, 4, p. 55.

5. *Ibid.,* II, 6, p. 40.

6. *Ibid.,* I, 5, pp. 15 - 16.

7. *Ibid.,* III, 4, pp. 52 - 53.

8. *Ibid.,* III, 5, pp. 56 - 57.

9. Cf. Emile Ripert, *op. cit.,* p. 54.

10. Cf. Elly Katz, *op. cit.,* pp. 32 - 33.

11. *Ibid.,* p. 38.

12. Norman, *op. cit., The Princess Far Away,* II, 3, p. 89.

13. *Ibid.,* III, 6, p. 116.

14. *Ibid.,* p. 117.

15. *Ibid.,* p. 119.

16. *Ibid.,* pp. 123, 124.

17. *Ibid.,* II, 3, p. 93.

18. *Ibid.,* I, 3, p. 73.

19. *Ibid.,* I, 2, pp. 70 - 71.

20. Norman, *op. cit., The Woman of Samaria,* I, 5, pp. 169 - 70.

21. *Ibid.,* I, 4, p. 161.

22. *Ibid.,* I, 5, p. 169.

23. *Ibid.,* III, 1, p. 195.

24. *Ibid.,* II, 3, p. 181.

Chapter Four

1. An interesting case of identification and empathy with the wounded Christian of Neuvillette is analyzed in C. G. Jung, *Symbols of Transformation. An Analysis of the Prelude to a Case of Schizophrenia* (New York, 1956), pp. 34 ff., which includes Jung's interpretation of the character of Cyrano. At the moment when Christian is killed and Sarah Bernhardt throws herself upon him to stanch the bleeding of his wound, Jung's patient felt a real, piercing pain in her own breast, just where Christian was supposed to have received the blow. But the tragic intermezzo with Christian is

played against a background of far wider significance, namely Cyrano's unrequited love for Roxane. According to Jung, the identification with Christian is probably only a cover.

2. Norman, *op. cit.*, *Cyrano of Bergerac*, V, 6, p. 360.

3. Elly Katz, *op. cit.*, p. 59.

4. Rosemonde Gérard, *Edmond Rostand* (Paris, 1935), pp. 10 - 12.

5. Norman, *op. cit.*, *Cyrano of Bergerac*, p. 209.

6. *Ibid.*, I, 4, pp. 233 - 35.

7. *Ibid.*, III, 11, pp. 303, 304, 305, 306 - 07.

8. *Ibid.*, I, 5, p. 241.

9. *Ibid.*, III, 6, p. 295.

10. *Ibid.*, V, 5, p. 352.

11. *Ibid.*, V, 6, p. 357.

12. *Ibid.*, IV, 8, p. 334.

13. *Ibid.*, V, 6, p. 358.

14. *Ibid.*, V, 2, p. 347.

15. Patricia Williams, "Some Classical Aspects of *Cyrano de Bergerac*," XIX Century French Studies, I, 2 (Winter 1973), 116.

16. T. S. Eliot, *Selected Essays 1917 - 1932* (New York, 1932), pp. 25, 28, 29.

17. Maria Luisa Rizzatti, "L'Aiglon: mito e verità," *Storia Illustrata*, XII, 123 (Feb. 3, 1968), 99.

18. *Ibid.*, 96 - 106.

19. Emile Ripert, *op. cit.*, p. 115.

20. Norman, *op. cit.*, dedication preceding *The Eaglet*.

21. Norman, *op. cit.*, p. 204.

22. *Ibid.*, *The Eaglet*, III, 1, p. 89.

23. *Ibid.*, V, 5, p. 180.

24. *Ibid.*, VI, 1, p. 191.

25. *Ibid.*, VI, 2, p. 194.

26. *Ibid.*, VI, 3, p. 196.

27. *Ibid.*, VI, 3, p. 198.

28. *Ibid.*, I, 13, p. 45.

29. *Ibid.*, IV, 7, p. 137.

30. *Ibid.*, VI, 3, p. 197.

31. *Ibid.*, II, 2, p. 55.

32. *Ibid.*, V, 5, pp. 181 - 82.

33. *Ibid.*, I, 9, p. 32.

34. *Ibid.*, V, 3, p. 175.

35. *Ibid.*, I, 13, p. 45.

36. *Ibid.*, III, 3, p. 97.

Chapter Five

1. Cited in J. W. Grieve, *op. cit.*, p. 76.
2. Norman, *op. cit.*, *Chanticleer*, Prelude, pp. 213, 214.
3. *Ibid.*, I, 4, p. 240.
4. *Ibid.*, I, 2, p. 225.
5. *Ibid.*, I, 4, p. 238.
6. *Ibid.*, I, 2, p. 227.
7. *Ibid.*, II, 3, p. 281.
8. *Ibid.*, pp. 288 - 89.
9. *Ibid.*, II, 1, p. 264.
10. *Ibid.*, I, 6, p. 250.
11. *Ibid.*, II, 3, p. 282.
12. *Ibid.*
13. *Ibid.*, II, 3, p. 290.
14. *Ibid.*, III, 4, p. 317.
15. *Ibid.*, pp. 319 - 20.
16. *Ibid.*, III, 5, p. 325.
17. *Ibid.*, IV, 2, p. 343.
18. *Ibid.*, IV, 3, p. 348.
19. *Ibid.*, IV, 6, p. 362.
20. *Ibid.*
21. *Ibid.*, IV, 7, p. 363.
22. *Ibid.*, p. 365.
23. *Ibid.*, p. 368.
24. *Ibid.*, IV, 8, p. 369.
25. *Ibid.*, II, 3, pp. 279, 285.
26. *Ibid.*, pp. 279, 280.
27. *Ibid.*, IV, 7, p. 367.
28. Emile Ripert, *op. cit.*, p. 156.
29. Cf. J. W. Grieve, *op. cit.*, p. 90, and Elly Katz, *op. cit.*, p. 86.
30. Cf. J. W. Grieve, *op. cit.*, p. 89.
31. Albert Camus uses the concept and form of the *auto sacremental* in *L'Etat de siège*. Belonging to the religious theater of the Spanish Golden Age, the *auto sacremental* represents in dramatic form abstract ideas in order to illustrate particular aspects of dogma. Much use is made of allegory with characters, who represent human types, facing forces such as Pity, Charity, or the Devil. The plays are essentially didactic and have other recurring characteristics such as tendentious speeches, grandiloquence, alternation in style between lyricism and the language of propaganda, elements of farce, and an easily discernible morality. (From *Forces in Modern French Drama, Studies in Variations on the Permitted Lie*, ed. by John Fletcher [New York: Frederick Ungar Publishing Co., 1972], *passim.*)

32. *The Last Night of Don Juan,* translated by T. Lawrason Riggs, in *Poetic Drama,* ed. by Alfred Kreymborg (New York, 1941), The First Part, p. 706.

33. *Ibid.,* p. 707.

34. *Ibid.*

35. *Ibid.,* p. 708.

36. *Ibid.,* p. 711.

37. *Ibid.,* p. 714.

38. *Ibid.,* The Second Part, p. 715.

39. *Ibid.*

40. *Ibid.,* p. 716.

41. *Ibid.,* p. 721.

42. *Ibid.*

43. *Ibid.,* pp. 721, 722.

44. *Ibid.,* p. 723.

45. *Ibid.*

46. *Ibid.*

47. *Ibid.,* p. 725.

Chapter Six

1. J. W. Grieve, *op. cit.,* p. 103.

2. *Discours de réception à l'Académie Française le 4 juin 1903* (Paris, 1903).

3. *Ibid.*

4. J. W. Grieve, *op. cit.,* pp. 118 - 19.

5. *Ibid.,* p. 128.

6. *Ibid.,* p. 131.

7. *Ibid.,* p. 132.

8. Norman, *op. cit., The Eaglet,* I, 2, p. 11.

9. Norman, *op. cit., The Princess Far Away,* III, 6, p. 117.

10. Norman, *op. cit., Chanticleer,* I, 6, p. 249.

11. *Ibid.,* I, 7, p. 254.

12. *Ibid.,* Prelude, p. 213.

13. *Ibid,* III, 4, p. 319.

14. Norman, *op. cit., Cyrano of Bergerac,* V, 6, p. 358.

15. Norman, *op. cit., Romantics,* I, 10, p. 21.

16. Norman, *op. cit., The Woman of Samaria,* III, 2, p. 199.

17. Norman, *op. cit., Cyrano of Bergerac,* I, 4, pp. 228, 229.

18. *Ibid.,* p. 235.

19. Norman, *op. cit., The Eaglet,* V, 2, p. 172.

20. *Ibid.,* III, 3, p. 100.

21. *Ibid.,* VI, 3, p. 200.

22. Norman, *op. cit.*, *The Princess Far Away*, III, 7, p. 124.

23. Norman, *op. cit.*, *The Woman of Samaria*, II, 3, p. 184.

24. Norman, *op. cit.*, *The Eaglet*, V, 5, p. 187.

25. *Ibid.*, IV, 7, p. 138.

26. Norman, *op. cit.*, *The Princess Far Away*, II, 7, p. 105.

27. Norman, *op. cit.*, *Chanticleer*, I, 2, p. 221.

28. *Ibid.*, II, 3, pp. 283 - 84.

29. Norman, *op. cit.*, *Cyrano of Bergerac*, IV, 3, p. 315.

30. Norman, *op. cit.*, *Chanticleer*, II, 1, p. 267.

31. *Ibid.*, IV, 1, p. 342.

32. Norman, *op. cit.*, *The Woman of Samaria*, I, 5, p. 170.

33. Norman, *op. cit.*, *The Princess Far Away*, II, 3, p. 91.

34. Norman, *op. cit.*, *Chanticleer*, IV, 6, p. 357.

35. Norman, *op. cit.*, *Cyrano of Bergerac*, II, 6, p. 259.

36. Norman, *op. cit.*, *The Woman of Samaria*, I, 4, p. 160.

37. Norman, *op. cit.*, *The Princess Far Away*, III, 3, p. 108.

38. Norman, *op. cit.*, *The Eaglet*, II, 9, p. 80.

39. Norman, *op. cit.*, *Chanticleer*, III, 4, p. 317.

40. Norman, *op. cit.*, *Cyrano of Bergerac*, IV, 6, p. 326.

41. Patricia Williams, loc. cit., pp. 120 - 21.

42. Louis Haugmard, *op. cit.*, p. 44.

43. J. W. Grieve, *op. cit.*, pp. 156 - 57.

44. Ernest Charles, cited in J. W. Grieve, *op. cit.*, p. 161.

45. André Gide, cited in Elly Katz, *op. cit.*, p. 95.

Selected Bibliography

PRIMARY SOURCES

L'Aiglon. Paris: Charpentier et Fasquelle, 1903.
Le Cantique de l'aile. Paris: Charpentier et Fasquelle, 1926.
Chantecler. Paris: Charpentier et Fasquelle, 1910.
Cyrano de Bergerac. Paris: Charpentier et Fasquelle, 1930.
Cyrano de Bergerac. Translated and Adapted for the Modern Stage by
    Anthony Burgess. New York: Knopf, 1971.
Cyrano de Bergerac. A New Version in English Verse by Brian Hooker,
    prepared for Walter Hampden. New York: Henry Holt & Co., 1923.
Cyrano de Bergerac. Translated from the French by Charles Renauld, with
    an introduction by Adolphe Cohn. New York: Frederick A. Stokes Co.,
    1899.
La Dernière Nuit de Don Juan. Paris: Charpentier et Fasquelle, 1921.
Les Deux Pierrots. Paris: Charpentier et Fasquelle, [1891].
Discours de réception à l'Académie Française le 4 juin 1903. Paris:
    Charpentier et Fasquelle, 1903.
The Last Night of Don Juan. Translated by T. Lawrason Riggs. In *Poetic
    Drama*, ed. Alfred Kreymborg. New York: Modern Age Books, 1941,
    pp. 702 - 25.
Les Musardises. Paris: Charpentier et Fasquelle, 1922.
Plays of Edmond Rostand. Translated by Henderson Daingerfield Nor-
    man. 2 vols. New York: Macmillan, 1921.
La Princesse lointaine. Paris: Charpentier et Fasquelle, 1908.
Les Romanesques. Paris: Charpentier et Fasquelle, 1917.
La Samaritaine. Paris: Charpentier et Fasquelle, 1920.
Un Soir à Hernani. Paris: Charpentier et Fasquelle, 1902.
Le Vol de la Marseillaise. Paris: Charpentier et Fasquelle, 1926.

SECONDARY SOURCES

APESTEGUY, PIERRE. *La Vie profonde d'Edmond Rostand*. Paris: Charpen-
    tier et Fasquelle, 1929. Rich collection of biographical anecdotes, with
    extensive commentary on Rostand's individual works.
BOILLOT, FÉLIX. "La Construction de la phrase dans *Cyrano de Bergerac*."
    Français moderne, Année 7 (1939), 301 - 16. Detailed stylistic study;

demonstrates Rostand's virtuosity in adapting his verses to the feelings
he wished to express.

DABADIÉ, MAÏTÉ. *Lettre à ma nièce sur Edmond Rostand, précédée d'une
lettre de Jean Rostand.* Toulouse: Privat, 1970. Contains some extremely revealing and useful biographical information.

ELIOT, T. S. *Selected Essays 1917 - 1932. New York: Harcourt, Brace, 1932.*
Essay on " 'Rhetoric' and Poetic Drama" demonstrates that *Cyrano of
Bergerac* satisfies the requirements of poetic drama. If the love scenes
in the play are dramatic speeches, then "rhetoric" covers good writing
as well as bad.

FAURE, PAUL. *Vingt ans d'intimité avec Edmond Rostand, avec une préface
de la Comtesse de Noailles.* Paris: Plon, 1928. Collection of anecdotes
of no particular usefulness for a literary study of Rostand's works.

GAUBER, CHARLES. *Impressions sur Chantecler.* Caen: Imprimerie A. Le
Boyteaux, 1911. Perceptive study of the similarities between
Chantecler and the medieval *Roman de Renart*, as well as between
Rostand and La Fontaine.

GÉRARD, ROSEMONDE. *Edmond Rostand.* Paris: Charpentier et Fasquelle,
1935. Collection of anecdotes by Rostand's wife, which explain the
genesis of many of his works.

GRIEVE. J. W. *L'Oeuvre dramatique d'Edmond Rostand.* Paris: Les
Oeuvres Représentatives, 1931. Outstanding critical study of Rostand's
works, with abundant and thoughtful commentary on each of his
plays.

HALE, EDWARD E., JR. *Dramatists of To-day.* New York: Holt & Co., 1905,
pp. 12 - 35. Short but good analysis of Rostand's realism.

HARTH, ERICA. *Cyrano de Bergerac and the Polemics of Modernity.* New
York and London: Columbia University Press, 1970. Analysis of the
works of the real Cyrano de Bergerac (1619 - 1655). Presents Cyrano as
a consistent flouter of authority, whose work is permeated with a
thoroughly modern spirit of satirical relativism.

HAUGMARD, LOUIS. *Edmond Rostand.* Paris: Sansot & Co., 1910. Contains a
biography, a criticism, a collection of opinions, and a bibliography of
Rostand's works. Evaluates Rostand as a poet and not a writer, because
he has failed to capture Beauty in its simplicity and serenity. Claims
that Rostand's theater is based on an artificial "playing" technique.

JUNG, C. G. *Symbols of Transformation. An Analysis of the Prelude to a
Case of Schizophrenia.* New York: Pantheon Books, 1956. Studies in-
stances of subconscious creative imagination in a patient who experienced instantaneous autosuggestion at a performance of *Cyrano of
Bergerac.*

KATZ, ELLY. *L'Esprit français dans le théâtre d'Edmond Rostand.*
Toulouse: Imprimerie Régionale, 1934. A doctoral dissertation that

goes far in explaining the presence of the French spirit in Rostand's principal heroes. The author places Rostand somewhere between Classicism and Romanticism.

LAUTIER, ANDRÉ et KELLER, FERNAND. *Edmond Rostand: son oeuvre.* Paris: La Nouvelle revue critique, 1924. Analysis of Rostand's cult of the Beautiful.

MOFFETT, CLEVELAND. "The Essence of Rostand's Greatness." *Theatre*, I, 5 (July 1901), 10 - 11. Sees the greatness of Rostand in his intense passion for his work.

MOUROUSY, PAUL. "Edmond Rostand: La gloire et le panache." *Cahiers d'art et d'amitié*, no. 1 (1945), 59 - 79. Assortment of biographical anecdotes presented with some personal recollections. The author sees France as Rostand's poetic Muse.

PAGE, DOROTHY. *Edmond Rostand et la légende napoléonienne dans l'Aiglon.* Paris: Champion, 1928. Excellent study of concordance and discordance between the Napoleonic legend and truth.

RENOUARD, DOMINIQUE. "Le romantisme d'Edmond Rostand." *Nouvelle revue*, sér. 4, tome 112 (1931), 25 - 40, Penetrating study of Rostand and the spirit of French heroism in his principal characters.

RIPERT, ÉMILE. *Edmond Rostand.* Paris: Hachette, 1968. Best critical biography of Rostand available.

RIZZATTI, MARIA LUISA. "L'Aiglon: mito e verità." *Storia Illustrata*, XII, 123 (Feb. 3, 1968), 96 - 106. Relates the historical background of *The Eaglet*, which helps to distinguish what parts of Rostand's play are based on fact, what part on legend, and the elements he created himself.

SMITH, HUGH E. *Main Currents of Modern French Drama.* New York: Holt & Co., 1925, pp. 76 - 107. Places Rostand in the current of idealistic literature.

SPIERS, A. G. H. "Rostand as Idealist." *Columbia University Quarterly*, 20 (1918), 155 - 69. Good analysis of Rostand's literary enthusiasm and his cult of the flamboyant (*le panache*). Sees the plays as an expression of devotion to a lofty ideal and a reflection of France's heroic attitudes in the war years.

WILLIAMS, PATRICIA. "Some Classical Aspects of *Cyrano de Bergerac*." *XIX Century French Studies*, I, 2 (1973). Relates *Cyrano de Bergerac* to the Aristotelian precepts of tragedy; demonstrates that *Cyrano* is a classical work principally because it is *plausible*.

Index

(The works of Rostand are listed under his name)